This book is dedicated to all

Small Press People

who labor long in humane causes
and who dream high.

AMERICAN ODYSSEY

A Bookselling Travelogue

By Len Fulton
with Ellen Ferber

$4.50/paper — **ISBN 0-913218-47-2**

$7.95/cloth — **ISBN 0-913218-46-4**

© 1975 Len Fulton
Ellen Ferber

Library of Congress Cataloging in Publication Data

FULTON, LEN.
  American odyssey, a bookselling travelogue.
    1. Booksellers and bookselling—United States—Colportage, subscription, trade, etc.
    2. Fulton, Len. The grassman.
    3. United States—Description and travel—1960.
  I. Ferber, Ellen, 1939—joint author.
  II. Title.
  HF5456.B8F844   658.8-09-0705730924 (B)
  ISBN 0-931218-46-4 ; 7525600

First Printing, 1975

"American Dust" Series, No. 1

Published by Dustbooks,
P.O. Box 1056, Paradise, CA 95969

COVER AND ILLUSTRATIONS

    by DAVID RAYMOND

BACK COVER PHOTO

    by LEONARD RANDOLPH

CONTENTS

Foreword by Ellen Ferber — 9

I. American Odyssey 74 — 11

II. Californicating Oregon — 21

III. Of Vladimir and Custer — 31

IV. Grass — 41

V. Winds & Walls — 47

VI. East of Ninety-Eight — 57

VII. Gravity's Zero (by Ellen Ferber) — 65

VIII. Green Skies — 73

IX. Discounts and Dimes — 87

X. Rivertown — 95

XI. Cornbasket — 103

XII. The Eye of the Sun — 113

Appendix A: Trip Summary — 121

Appendix B: Annotated List of Bookstores — 131

Subject Index — 169

Index to Bookstores — 177

Foreword

What's a nice (I mean born and raised in the Big Apple, in big houses with tables just to put flower vases on) girl (woman with a professional commitment, table manners and flyers for tax sheltered annuities arriving in the mail) like you (upper-middle-class, urban, good schools) doing (filling out orders on cheap order blanks, picked up here and there at stationery stores) on a trip like (10,000 miles in a car with stops for store-to-store selling and late night cheap motels, the back seat littered with cartons of flyers and books) this?

This book and the trip it chronologues are the results of a unique energy, American in essence, populist in shape. The energy itself belongs to the individual/tribal pulse of small press-people, and to Len Fulton, for whom the idea of selling his novel, *The Grassman*, directly and personally to the bookstores was the completion of his obsession to be part of the total process of literature in America.

The market place is America's measure of value. As Eudora Welty's wise child taunts, "If you're so smart, why ain't you rich?" Honoring your bladder in much of this country demands, not just ten cents, but A DIME. The market place, if arbitrary, is very exacting. You can, if you dream, or love literature, art or other hard to move items, be destroyed by it, like that famous All-American, Jay Gatsby. You can opt out, push into the land and do without it. Or, you can, as it was Len's idea to do, try to humanize it. You can try to hone, to tailor the measure to your values.

The feeling logic of small presses demands the last of these. An editor of *The New York Times Book Review* once said that small presses were not intrinsically interesting because anyone could start one (unlike, the corollary goes, commercial houses, which can only be started by people with money). Small Presses are interesting because they are started by readers who put American currency behind their love of contemporary literature, not just coin, but energy. Small press publishing is a style of life.

I don't know any small press publishers who don't hope that a book they publish will sell, but I don't know any who accept a manuscript simply because they think it will. But what to do with that hope, since one of the ironies of the market place is that it takes money, not only to make a book, but also to sell it: money for advertising in review journals, money for free copies to seed the ground, money for cocktail parties and meet the authors? The only other legal tender is the energy of belief in the literature. Small presspeople cannot afford the luxury of disdain, of scorning to cast their pearls before swine. They need to cultivate an American taste for pearls. It cannot be done with the long handled hoe, and even if it would work, we couldn't afford a cultivator.

So, we sold books in bookstores, sometimes one at a time, and sometimes none. It was a process to drive market researchers mad. We also gave them away, bartered and traded with them and with talk about them. And we saw America, in parking lots and toilets, in malls and dry washes, on highways, in cities, on ridges, through trees. Then, as we relived it, talking, filling orders, sending flyers, this book was written.

I had never sold, not girl scout cookies, not anything, before. I was afraid of it, and was shamed at my relief when there was only one store in walking distance and I could sit and wait hopefully in the car. I had no special talent for it, and I'm not much good at it even yet. It got easier, but I don't know now if it would be any easier if I started out to do it again. But it was worth doing and, easier or not, it would be worth doing again. So long as Americans opt for the market place, people will have to get out there and keep the place clean.

—ELLEN FERBER
PARADISE
JUNE, 1975

I. American Odyssey 74

On June 18, 1974, Ellen Ferber and I struck north up the spine of California. Before it was over, we'd traveled through Oregon, into Washington, eastward across the northern midwest to and through New England—and back. The trip, by car, lasted seven weeks. We covered 9,900 miles, some twenty-four states, and negotiated the often mean centers of more than 65 American cities with populations from 25,000 to 540,000. The first purpose of the trip was to put my novel, *The Grassman* (which had just been published by Thorp Springs Press) into bookstores across the country, along with, if possible, the new (Tenth) Edition of the *International Directory of Little Magazines and Small Presses*, the *Whole COSMEP Catalog**, and other Dustbooks' titles. Second, and quite unavoidably in fact, we promoted small, independent publishing, do-it-yourselfism, contemporary literature, and non-corporate-giant endeavors of several kinds. We visited more than 250 bookstores, many libraries and wholesale distributors, and a string of newspaper reviewers. We started with a car bowed under the weight of books, and sold them all by the time we reached Sundance, Wyoming, keeping only copies enough to use for taking further orders. In New York we picked up a new load, and then another in Massachusetts, all of which were gone by Pittsburgh, coming back. In the immediate sense we sold about 500 copies of *The Grassman*, 200 of the *Directory*, and dozens of assorted other titles, including of course the *Whole COSMEP Catalog*. In the longer-term sense we "opened" some seventy-five new bookstores as accounts, set many others to pondering, and compiled a hell of a list of stores, with annotations. Furthermore, we rooted out reviewers on newspapers across the country, some quite amazingly receptive to small-press titles—especially if, after coming all that way, we cared enough still about seeing them to buck police guards in the lobby and dive through two or three departments to find them. What follows here is a kind of summary of that trip, some notions about it—before, during and after— as a Chapter One.

---
* COSMEP = Committee of Small Magazine Editors and Publishers, a San Francisco based organization of 750 Small Presses. The *Catalog* was a 300-page, 11x14 book I published on behalf of the org's members.

* * *

In twelve years of publishing I had always wanted to do this. There was something *steamy* and *vital* to the fact that this country was as jammed as any in the world with places where the printed word was merchandised, where the reader walked among quiet or crowded shelves and found something he or she wanted badly enough to barter for. Oh hell, I know it's not the best of all possible bookstore worlds out there in Amerikka; a dozen years of publishing new literature by *living writers* has revealed some measure of its defect, and I'm sure there are other places where better things abide. But I had inherited that marketplace, had contributed to it (always conscionably, I thought), and wanted to visit it. The artist was the bicep, the publisher the forearm, the bookstore the fingers which touch out to what will be touched. Many times I had verged on getting a van and going out to those fingers, but something always intervened—time, money, you know.

Several events conspired to make this the year to do it, if not an indefinite and exhaustive journey, at least some summer weeks. One event was, of course, the publication of *The Grassman*, a western saga whose life and continuity had been for me a sixteen year affair, whose people had become my own children demanding to take their freedom (else turn to caged devils in my heart). Once the deal was made with Foreman and Thorp Springs I fussed until that smooth green paperback with Andy Curry's incredible cover looked down on me—and all traces of anal jealousy departed. It deserved, as a novel, a renewed effort now, a slap on the ass, a suckle, a full blood-run to the ends of the fingers. I had said often, and know now the pure rightness of that notion, that a book's best salesman is its author, that one who shares all the continuity.

Another event was the seventh COSMEP Conference in July in New York City, for me an annual tribal renewal, a revitalizing of parts and energies, a dance, not always holy to be sure, of the small press community. I leave to others their courses; for me COSMEP, to whose genesis I gave blood, requires annual visiting. This year too was the jointly sponsored COSMEP-ALA (American Library Association) Book Fair in New York, magnificently managed by Jackie Eubanks, and which attracted, as it turned out, more than 15,000 visitors in three days.

There was also, and finally, for both Ellen and myself, the simple need to be on some road, away for awhile from production, packaging and postage. We had put the Dustbooks imprint on about two dozen projects in the year, not the least of which was the massive *Whole COSMEP Catalog* in January, and the huge Tenth *Directory* in May. We had been staring through light tables, opaquing negatives, proofreading galleys, lugging cartons of books and magazines for months, and Ellen had been teaching, too, full time. The need was not to "get away from books and publishing" but to explore extensions of that, to somehow get free for awhile of the demanding machinery of production and fulfillment while working in the cause. Distribution is, of course, the final, vital step in that cause.

Not to put too fine a point on it, selling seems to me about the hardest work a body can do. The process consumes energy like a great sponge. I'm convinced almost no one really likes it in the same sense one likes to print or to spread manure on a winter field. Back in New England once I tried encyclopaedias, and took time enough to note that you either had to be a show-off kid or a drunk, if you would do it as a living. Selling has no golden middle ground that I can see. It has no point of rest. Its root in the medulla oblongata is tension and vulnerability—you are always vulnerable whether you are selling or being sold.

No sooner had we raised the great white cone of Mt. Shasta on the upper right horizon than that process we'd called "distribution" defined itself, quite simply and almost purely, as *selling*. Nor can I say that from Red Bluff, California, where we started, to Tahoe City, California, where we quit, that I ever got toughened to it, or that it became easier to climb up my own psyche—sometimes before morning coffee—and talk my body through that first door. With books the work is made harder by the fact that independent bookstores lie almost universally at city centers, which means plunging through morning, noon, or late afternoon traffic, parking somehow without walking endlessly—because the more time you spend on foot the fewer stores you get to, and the worse you look when you arrive. There are in this country's cities some palatial malls, shopping plazas, modern, air-conditioned canyons which spring like mirages from asphalt deserts. These are tempting for easy access—but beware. Certain huge chains like Dalton and Walden have staked these mirages out for their own, and such stores only rarely will order individually. You have to go to Minneapolis (Dalton) or Stamford, Connecticut (Walden) or some other place and talk to sources. The Walden chain is in fact a case in point because I visited perhaps a dozen of them personally with no luck whatever while Paul Foreman, the *Grassman*'s publisher, arrived at the source—and took an immediate order for more than a hundred.

Anyway, as to the inner trials of selling, small games help, and small, knowing sensibilities, oft-repeated along the sidewalk. As:
1) These outfits would die without writers and publishers; so
2) They are in great need and want of what I have here, for
3) How could they not desire this incredible book?
4) I'm just traveling around really, you know, an *author visiting* stores telling them about his new book.
5) (Macho) I'm tougher'n they are—charge!
6) (Astronaut psychology) I'm out here, 1275 miles into it, so what else is there?
7) (superego ploy) I'll feel guilty if I *don't*.
8) They can't do more'n kill.

Ellen took a few good stabs at it too, and revealed her most-used one:
9) I'm not really here.

In all, though, it was not that hard. We were book people talking to book people about books, and we learned as much or more than we taught. It was human contact of the sort we valued, out at those fingers which touch the reader, in Corvallis, in Coeur d'Alene, Big Timber, Sioux Falls, and Montpelier. For every kneejerk proprietor there were ten who cared about what they were doing, ten to whom books were not just merchandise but a way of life, a bearing on human intelligence, sensibility, and worth. Hard as some of the work was, and grinding as the miles, it was more than worth the journey.

We quickly developed a kind of "road strategy" for we knew we had just under three weeks to make New York City—where we would spend five days at the Book Fair and COSMEP Conference. We wanted to visit Spokane's Expo '74, and spend some hours photographing the Thunder Basin area of northeastern Wyoming, the setting for *The Grassman*—an area that is about to be criminally strip-mined for its bituminous coal deposits. So we did have to make progress eastward. The road strategy was guided by the fact that bookstores are 9 to 5 operations, with that period from

11:30 to 1:30 very chancy because of lunch time—especially for managers and book buyers, who tend toward two-hour meals. This leaves an effective 6-hour day, ideally split to work one city in the morning and one in the afternoon, with noontime for travel. It rarely panned out that way, of course. In Montana though it did. We arrived in Missoula in the evening, visited the stores the next morning, and raced 116 miles to Butte for the afternoon. That evening we drove the 100 miles to Bozeman to work it, and Billings 130 miles farther along the next day. That plan jelled elsewhere too: in Syracuse and Buffalo, Iowa City and Des Moines, Omaha and Lincoln. Such mileage planning would seem more critical in the open west where everything is a hundred miles from everything else. But in the east traffic problems, the multiplicity of routes, and congested, maze-like inner cities equalize the west's distance. So planning is still important. In Middletown (N.Y.), or Pittsburgh, the main city streets are quaintly narrow and sometimes formidable. Again, as on the sidewalk, you climb your psyche—and drive into it. Madness awaits those who do not develop a compensatory attitude toward city traffic. You flirt always with that madness *whatever* you do: We came into Hartford one rainy night, entering from the west and searching for the interstate going north. New England rather unnerves me in a basic way, but here was wet weather, bad twisty streets, confusion of routes, and cars bearing down and all around, giving no quarter whatever to an out-of-stater. "I remember these bastards," I heard myself to say through tight teeth, and calling the first 25 years of my life up across my consciousness. "OK, they want DRIVING? I'll give them DRIVING like it is in CALIFORNIA!"

The road strategy also included cheap motels most of the time, though we were packing camping gear. Camping, however, is a process in itself, demanding more attention and time than we had to give. We drove late into virtually every night, and were in no mood as a rule for paraphernalia. And campgrounds are not as cheap as they once were, nor particularly plentiful. In the summer months they fill up before anything else—with a certain grossness transported fresh from the cities. Yet another piece of the strategy was not to visit along the way. This was especially hard for me because in the many years of publishing information about small presses I've come to value friendships in almost any town you please. It is part in fact of the strength of the small press movement that it is geographically dispersed, and here as we moved through towns and cities where I knew a small press or two operated I was *feeling* that dispersal. Well, this part of the strategy was calculated always to be saddening (and it broke down a few times)—but we knew, again that the particular energy we were using, and the *time*, was precious and finite. Maybe with three months the thing could be different. Maybe next year....

We developed a street tactic, a way of going once we were at the edge of a city. We discovered we would always need two things immediately: a city street map, and a list of bookstores. Motels often had rudimentary copies of the former (and rudimentary was usually enough), and the yellow pages contained most of the latter. If we arrived in a city the night before we would plot our position and locate the stores as we decadently watched the tailend of the Carson show. The morning then was easier. If we arrived on the afternoon leg, Ellen (whose handwriting was both clearer and quicker) went for a phone book while I chased down a map. This whole operation was best done in a mall or shopping center *outside* the main city, because then we could plot our way into it street by street. We discovered that to head directly for what we thought was a city center committed us to unnecessary (and often uncorrectible) errors, and parking problems. We stayed too long in La Crosse, for example, and by the time we had driven 150 miles to Madison it was 4 PM and we faced a city of more than 170,000. But we did it right, stopped at a plaza on the way in, spread the map on the car hood and spent five minutes plotting, covering, as it turned out, the major bookstores (a dozen). In Buffalo (pop. 462,000) we played it backwards, found ourselves imprisoned in a massive downtown mall (with no toilet facilities except those in the mall restaurants which required a dime to get through the door) and had to battle 4:30 traffic street-for-street up to the university area five miles away. We missed half the city's sixteen prospective stores, though ironically sold many more books there than in Madison. The midwest, north and south and generally, was as tough as dried-up corn, from Rapid City east, and Columbus west.

If I made errors in approaching a given store it was on the side of the hayseed. Mostly, though, I found it less taxing to simply be myself, and get the attention shifted as quickly as possible to the copy of *The Grassman*, which I usually carried in both its green paperback form and in cloth, with the stark white dustjacket. "Would you be interested in carrying copies of my new book?" I would say, laying the copies before them—and revealing at that point that I also carried the *Directory*, as well as an order book at the very bottom of the deck. I would pack a Dustbooks brochure in my back pocket, and often also have other propaganda slung into the order book. Sometimes too I would have the *Whole COSMEP Catalog*, or other Dustbooks, under my arm. But there is a limit just how much you can haul into a place and expect attention. I had begun by carrying a large briefcase, but started to feel (and, I swear, *look*) like an encyclopaedia salesman, and few bookstore people seemed willing to plow through everything in it. For that sort of "heavier" selling you need appointments, time—you need to be in the business of it up to your ears. For me it was a quick two or three-title thing, and if their attention held I would then lead them through the Dustbooks brochure. It happened, more often than I would have expected, that they wanted several titles; but it also happened, and I could feel it in the air, that their limit from a "new house" was one or two titles. Fair enough. I discovered also that a certain careful timing was required in pushing objects at people. Many seemed a little frail in this, would flinch if I unloaded my wares too abruptly upon them; others were hungerers whose eyes (and hands) reached out to take. Several times in fact the order book itself was grabbed away! I found there was a moment after I handed them the first book, while the mind was still in motion and un-made-up, that was the optimum for easing the other things into their vision. So that as they digested my own presence and purpose, and copies of *The Grassman*, I would lay the *Directory* out too, and mumble, "I also publish this every year." I don't want to belabor this point, but I found it absolutely critical to get everything out during that moment of mental motion so that everything would be considered in the decision process. This moment runs from seven to twelve seconds on the average, and if you wait for a decision on the first offering it is ten times harder to introduce the second. People often make a second decision (I find this true of myself with my own son) based not on exterior logic or circumstances but on a kind of one-way mental Hegelian Dialectic. If they decide *yes* once they will decide *no* a second time. Once or twice I got a *no* on *The Grassman* and a *yes* on the *Directory*, but that was rare—which is what I mean by "one-way."

Waiting in New York was a copy of Gene Detro's gorgeous review in the *Oregon Journal* which compared *The Grassman* to Steinbeck's *To A God Unknown*. We carried copies of that before us all the way back, and that didn't hurt a whisker. In Agawam, Massachusetts, I rapped for two hours about the book and about small publishing in general to a totally responsive and attentive audience jammed into the public library; in Syracuse Walt Shepperd, Joe Bruchac and I set up a table on the street and sold enough books to throw a party that night; in Pittsburgh Anne Pride, the president of an incredible women's publishing collective known as KNOW, arranged two TV shows and a newspaper interview—and also, with her husband Ed (a silkscreen printer) opened home and heart to us. There were downers, too, outright bummers—like my old home town of Portland, Maine, whose crusty ways change for no wind or water.

In short, it was ten thousand miles of America, the high and low of it, and mostly the in between.

The following eleven chapters track those miles.

II. Californicating Oregon

Oregon is a land of mythic dimension. It rises like a dream in the northwest of the continent with all that a dream can hold of rivers, mountains and plains. The Pacific, the Columbia, the Snake are its borderwaters, and Hood in the north stands like a medicine sentinel-woman watching down the Willamette and across the Siskiyous to the storm of civilization rolling up from the south. Oregon has 100,000 square miles and two million people; California has 160,000 square miles and twenty million people. That's 20 per square mile in Oregon, 125 in California. The largest city in Oregon is Portland with fewer than 400,000 people, Eugene and Salem have around 70,000 apiece, and all the rest of Oregon's cities are considerably smaller than 50,000. By contrast California has several jittery urban complexes of over a million, smog problems in a dozen places or more, traffic, crime, and ecological suicide going forward from the destruction of Riverside County agriculture to the Santa Barbara oil spillage and the pollution of Lake Tahoe. California has continued in this century to pack the deserts of its southland with people, and drain the northland of its water to support them. As a river goes so goes the quality of life all about it, and Oregonians—with trouble enough thank you on the mighty Columbia and the Willamette—eye the lowering of northern California waters with rightful alarm. Who *are* those guys anyway? How long before the Klamath is tapped? How long the Rogue?

You travel over the whole continent and you know, you know as sure as the Snake has water and Hood snow, that once the northern Rockies fall to stripmining—as they are falling—the northwest is the end of it for America. There is a bumper sticker that tells the mood—"Don't Californicate Oregon."

Oregon is the land of Ken Kesey and Don Berry. It possesses a literacy and a sense of its literary *self* as no other place I've visited. Poets and writers abound—Gene Detro, Walt Curtis, Marjorie, Marty Cohen, Marty Christensen, Vi Gale, Dick Bakken and many many others keep the scene alive and moving and open. Poets like

Gary Elder, Ben Hiatt and Ron Bayes are Oregon natives, and too I'm reminded of the early and mid-sixties northwest small press scene—Hiatt's *Grande Ronde Review*, Carlos Reyes' *Pliego*, Jerry Paul Simpson's *Aspects*, all in Oregon; and Jan Kepley's *Mad Virgin*, Mel Buffington's *Blitz*, Charles Potts' *Litmus*, from Seattle.

Ellen Ferber and I passed through Oregon twice this summer, once in June selling, once again in August to attend the Second Annual Portland Poetry Festival. In June we were just getting our sidewalk legs, our driving, book baggage and such coordinated. The first day we hit only two stores, one in Red Bluff, California, at the northern edge of the Sacramento Valley, and one at Redding, farther up the spine. Middle Earth Books in Red Bluff was the moment of reality, the flash, in the heat of the day, that told me it would be a long and twisty trip; that the number-one obstacle would be other autos; that the heat and the noise and the rarified air *no* city is without, would rank close behind—and all would come before "bookstore resistance" or ignorance of small-press publishing. If bookstores were as easy to get to as Penny's or Sears, for example, this country would be quite a different place. I thought often on this trip that, given the vagaries of the Postal System on the one side, and inner-city traffic travails on the other, you could only come to a sense of love and admiration for book readers, for their determination and sacrifice. Middle Earth Books of Red Bluff was a small, cool haven out of the sunstorm, and as the proprietor and her daughter appraised *The Grassman* I grew twitchy, heard my psychic cage rattle some as I delivered up the *Directory of Little Mags and Small Presses*. At the same moment I also saw Bowker's boulder-sized *Books in Print* on a far counter, and as their interest increased on seeing the Directory I opened the Dustbooks brochure and began explaining our annual author/title index, the *Small Press Record*, and Glide's *Alternatives in Print*, which we also carry. I began to realize just how blasted *much* I knew about books and publishing, and what an unplanned and unaccountable *joy* it was to be sharing the knowledge, and taking related interest in their knowledge too. A great sense of my own usefulness infused the day, raised me up out of the cage. I remembered that booksellers were that outer ring of the tribe, and that books, unlike shoes, had yet another level of value beyond the physical, and that that value had a curious effect right at the market place. The effect was to enlarge human vision all around. It raised the level of negotiation between buyer and seller. I discovered that the *work* of it, the talk about books, was that very thing I most coveted as meaningful conversation, anytime. And I sold two Grassmans and two Directories, and got paid. I don't attack boulders, and I didn't then attack *Books in Print*, but on some subsequent occasions, with people who were a little hardcased about it (and because every bookcounter in the universe groans under *BIP*'s great weight) I would mention a small-press title or two, complete with author and date, and twiddle while they thumbed the big grey pages, not finding what I'd named. The real rock-crackers, of course, were broadsides like those of the Alternative Press (Detroit), or Skratz's Stone Press Weekly postcards, or those of Buffalo Joe Ribar.

The second day along we started off like new-cut gears with a sale to Trans Books in the mountain village of Yreka, and rumbled over the pass into Oregon. The town of Ashland, population 12,300, is the scene of the annual Shakespeare Festival, and home of Southern Oregon College. The Festival runs through August and September of every year, and the one performance I'd attended there (*Henry IV, Part II*) was so impressive that for some time thereafter I tried to coerce Ellen, a Shakespeare expert, into writing a series of pamphlets on it for the Dustbooks imprint. Ashland is plastered along the east face of the Siskiyous with Mount Ashland rising 7,500 feet behind. It is a comfortable town, but one you suspect might lag in its general intellect behind its internationally famous Festival. We visited six bookstores, found five managers out, sold nothing. We learned here of the 11:30 to 1:30 lunch hour, and developed a mental tactic for it that worked *some* of the time: no waiting around unless it suited the plan; no re-visits unless it was to our own convenience. Movement was to be the all-consuming plan—and no haunting regrets for rocks unturned. Hell, you wait enough as it is.

In Ashland the owner of the one good possibility, McCarley's, was on vacation (another summertime hazard) but his clerk led me to believe he'd be anxious to carry the Grassman. On the August trip I stopped again, and experienced one of the fastest moments of disinterest from McCarley of my whole, short selling career.

Depressed, not yet hardened to a full flunk-out, nor knowing what ultimate meaning to give it, we slipped into Medford a dozen miles up the line. Pop: 28,400—enough, you would guess, to balm any depression. Yet there were still only five stores—the same number as Ashland, and considerably more cars, torn-up streets and one-way alleys. Another raw discovery, then: population bears only a *slightly* direct relation to number of bookstores, and that a rather complex one. (Generally it is that the number of bookstores per thousand of population grows as the population shrinks, which is no big news as long as you remember that up to 40,000 a city is negotiable, and after that you flirt with madness. At 40,000 the number of stores per thousand is around .08; at 10,000 it is .15; at 175.000 it is below .07. Many factors affect this thing profoundly, such as the presence of a college or two. And, as you move away from either coast into the heartlands you encounter more and more Christian bookstores, which exist in some unexplainable fashion in inverse proportion to other, general stores.) Some of the news from Medford was hopeful: Booklands called *The Grassman* a "quality paperback" and hoped to stock it when newly located; Swems carried much western nonfiction in hardcover, and had a very knowledgeable manager who would "consider" the novel; and Bob and Jean Zaddock of Books Primarily (all used) were as cordial as any booksellers I met in 10,000 miles. A little desperate, running out of light, I visited the Jackson County Library reference person, a Mrs. Place who flashed an 8th *Directory* at me and guessed that was "probably up to date enough," all things considered. The wrap-up note for that day of June 19th was: "Bah!" No energy left to create a worthy expletive.

That night it rained a little in the Willamette Valley. A kind of cleansing drift rode down off the Columbia. Eugene had so many stores even a baboon would leave something behind! But we sat up late with city map and phone book and plotted that town right down to its socks. We went over the pitch ("a little more hayseed...dampen that impulse to brim with knowledge."), the sales luggage ("The briefcase is out."), and the footgear (the cowboy boots were shot; the Apache boots came out—"they'll have to un-mix the image for themselves, I got blisters!"). Next day we sold 23 *Grassman*s and 22 *Directories*, plus assorted other titles. I met an old customer, Son of Koobdooga Books, and finding someone who *knew* me after all those miles and more than a dozen stores was like coming to a waterhole of small press titles! There were 13 bookstores in Eugene, and we visited them all. At the University of Oregon Bookstore I took another short lesson in small matters: the woman out front sent me to the buyer out back, and I neglected to show the check-out clerks what I was taking in with me. When I confronted these clerks on the way out again we fell into a brief discussion about who owned the books I carried. I blew it like that a couple of other times, too, and eventually developed the habit of not going into a store until I had shown my wares to the cashier.

It began to be good, then. Next day, June 21st, we worked Corvallis, Albany and Salem, leaving a trail of books behind. That sense of spreading books, like seeds in the earth, began to be luscious, whatever the Freudian impulse behind it. Salem (68,300) was truculent with commerce and we faired not well there, but the last stop—Willamette University—decided to try the *Directory*. We then stood before Portland, and counted 28 bookstores—a day's work if you ever saw one.

Somewhere on the western apron of that great city we pulled into a shopping center to consider our supply of books and the distance left to us. We knew we would be returning to Portland in August. We had not yet even turned east toward New York. We were down to less than a hundred books, and we *had* to have some for northeastern Wyoming, a thousand miles away. So we decided to head up the Columbia to The Dalles, make Spokane by Saturday night and visit Expo '74 on Sunday, a dead day for bookselling anyway.

For the moment, though, we were hungry. We saw a sign in that shopping center which said *food*, and close to it another that said *books*. Next we knew we were in La Faye's Brindavan eating metaphysical clam chowder, and watching a "Brindavan Class" ("Astrology, numerology, tarot, palmistry, creative awareness, dream interpretation, color.") We said we were from California. They asked after our mission. We explained it. "Could we see that book?" they wanted to know. "I'm flattered to show you," I said (the chowder was hefty but good). "Bring five or so," someone called as I went out. *Five*? I thought. Saint Gawd! I brought five and signed them while five of the dozen or so people gathered came up and gave me $2.95 each. A nicer bunch didn't exist!

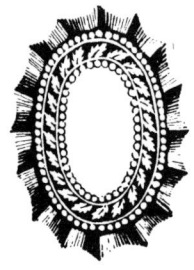

III. Of Vladimir and Custer

After the wide, dark, dammed waters of the Coumbia, Hood standing to the right like the nation's cornerblock, we pushed up the dry grasslands of eastern Washinton toward Spokane. We had stopped in The Dalles the night, left some books on consignment at Weigelt's, and finished the Saturday business hours in a fruitless struggle through the sweltering heat of Kennewick, Richland, and Pasco. These three cities lie stuffed together above the Columbia-Snake fork, and treacherously south of the Hanford Atomic Energy Reservation. Out of Richland north, nearer still to doom, the country grinds itself into a farinaceous powderchalk, until you begin to guess you've found hell. But no, off that desert of stray, high-speed neutrons rises a shopping mall—real because it stinks , and is noisy. We made the chase three times through these fiery cities in search of a bookstore owner, Mrs. Shields, and because we refused to believe that a combined population of 55,000 couldn't support more than two book outlets (a per-thousand ratio of .04). We were learning about that.

Spokane held promise. There were almost a dozen stores packed handily into the center of a city of 170,000—a city for the moment on an international cloud with Expo '74 sucking in thousands of travelers an hour. (And Carl Cletus Bowles, the escaped prisoner, had just been gunned down in the Spokane River, to add notoriety.) Expo was on an island in that pounding, awesome river. The Expo theme, *environment*, would seem to have meant educational, non-plastic, unhyped sincerity— and often this was the case. But when governments compete for the role of Savior you get propaganda, and you got plenty of that. Actually, the U.S. exhibit wasn't bad, a vast junkpile forty feet high surrounded by demonstrations of water-wasting, with some pseudo-totem poles stuck in to no good purpose. The Russian "pavilion" was an unabashed monument to glitter and gimmicks, architectural flounce, and claims to ecological heroism. Here, I managed to find a bookstore, however, which differed from the American one because it carried (cleverly) books without a "Dept. of This or That" imprint or sanction. The books anywhere on this island were

State-as-environmental-Savior business too, but in the Russian display I did see Yevtushenko and Mayakovsy included with Lenin and Brezhnev. I accosted a small, thin, shy man at the counter. He introduced himself as Vladimir.

"Do you have any anthologies of young, unkown Russian poets?"

He shook his head and was self-conscious.

"They are not translated."

"Why?" I asked steadily, thinking of Lifshin, Blazek, Wantling, thinking of how they'd look in Russian.

"Because Americans don't read poetry," he said quickly.

I thought to stick my finger out to him, but that portion of truth in his words held me down. I retrieved a Dustbooks brochure from my back pocket.

"Don't generalize about us too easily, Vladimir," I said weakly, handing him the brochure, and in my mind, as we chatted further, generalizing myself about the instinct of the Russian for popular, capital economics.

The day off at Expo softened us for the sidewalk on Monday. Spokane, we figured, with its new internationalism, would seize upon the cosmic *COSMEP Catalog* before we could get it out of the car, and as a town along the upper edge of the Old West it would see the immediate salability of *The Grassman* to natives and visitors alike. But the internationalism was mostly crammed onto that river island, and Spokane's image of itself was confused. Provincialism dies hard, even in the face of Russian heroes. Spokane's daily papers fixed safely on Expo's cosmetics: Who was responsible for the air-conditioning failure in the Philippine Pavilion? The Montana State Song made you cry. Attendance statistics were endlessly and obsessively tracked. We planted one pile of the novel and the *Directory*—no *Catalogs*—in the best place possible, John Graham Books on Riverside Avenue, but that was it. The Feminist Bookstore was closed on Monday as were some other stores, including Erewhon, an old mail customer. We hit summer vacations and a couple of flat noes (rare, until the midwest). We had miscued on the handiness of the city's belly, too, the width of its blocks, which was twice what we'd reckoned. The weight (2.31 pounds) of the *COSMEP Catalog* took its toll once again here, too, as it had at my Paradise place where I'd lugged cartons, 23 books in each, from storage to office to post office and truck all spring.

On the streets of Spokane I came to a sudden insight: You should never publish a book bigger than you're willing to carry. Stewart Brand, I suspected, must have muscles on his muscles—or hernias on his whatever. I mumbled this later to Jim Silberman, the Random House editor who'd bought the *Whole Earth Catalog* from Brand. Turns out Silberman never tried carrying a couple dozen at a time. And probably never walked the streets of Spokane with even one.

By this time we were learning to move out of turmoil. By midafternoon we were in Idaho, and in the last gasp of the business day filled up two of the three possibilities in Coeur d'Alene. A pharmacist named Wilson looked at the *Grassman*, opened his cash register and said, "How much?"—and a fine new store a block away was manifestly pleased to have small publishers visiting that northcountry. We headed across the Bitterroots for Missoula, watching the sun hang in the southwest as though the Russians had stopped its descent to prove all. It was in fact light until ten that evening, the way it is at the western edge of a time zone, but more dramatic there against the mighty sky. The mountains were cold and dark, white on the upper north faces. The road, much of it, was frost-heaved, pocked, and deadly.

Six hundred miles from end to end, Montana could be covered, bookselling, in about five days, most of it on the road (you'd drive 2,000 miles). We had two days, and hit four major and three minor towns, sold three dozen *Grassman*s and 25 or 30 other books. The best city on that route for us—and the most beautiful to the eye—was Bozeman, the upper end of the Montana Road, the home of Montana State University, with one of the largest, most progressive bookstores on any campus in the West. Missoula seemed uneasy and crowded, Butte was a depressed area (in spite of Evel Knievel), and Billings didn't appear to read—.05 stores per thousand as against Bozeman's .16 or better. The traffic in Billings was merciless, and the city splayed out like fresh calf dung on soft coal. In one small town, Big Timber in the Sweetwater country, we found a tiny store operated by a man named John Baird. Baird was a small publisher himself, Buckskin Press, and had issued (and printed) books on the old Hawken rifle and other facets of Montana heritage and craft. I traded him a copy of the *Directory* for his own mag, *The Buckskin Report*, and he played me a song on the dulcimer he'd just made out of a piece of wood from Indiana.

37

"I'll take copies of your novel," he said. "I know what you're up against." What about winter here on the Sweetwater?

"Hell, man," he said with the look of one who'd just crossed trails with a California sun farmer, "you ever spent a winter in Indiana?"

Except for its silver once, and now its coal, Montana would be a separate universe, curtained off by the white norther in January, the endless, uncharted green in July. But the silvermud blasted it into the Nineteenth Century, and the black, bituminous dust will draw it slogging into the Twentieth. Like Oregon wood, Montana coal seems destined to be ripped out for the big eaters of Chicago, Los Angeles, Tokyo. The Twentieth Century conscience chases you from the Kootenai all the way to the Rosebud.

And then out of Billings east and south, inside the Crow Reservation, another conscience lurks. We arrived as the sun dropped toward the edge of a flawless sky. We slipped past Custer Hill along what is known as Battlefield Road, which runs south by east for five miles to where Reno, Benteen and remnants of the Seventh Cavalry made their stand against the Cheyenne and Sioux on June 25th and 26th, 1876. Custer, on the 25th, had taken five companies, ridden down along the east side of the ridge into the Medicine Tail Coulee, out of it across Deep Coulee in an obvious effort to get round to the north of the Sioux-Cheyenne encampment along the Little Big Horn River. He turned west up the ridge again about five miles north, and topped out into the very teeth of the Indians, assaulting up the opposite side. No one survived of the Long Knives, but back at the Benteen-Reno site trenches were dug around the tailend of the ridge and a two-day siege ensued.

It was dusk, ninety-eight years later to the day, and we stood on the end of that ridge, the whole green, rolling slab of Montana spread out before us and darkening. All other beings had gone with the sun. Ghosts walked. They crouched, bellied and elbowed into shallow trenches. White ghosts shivered in the early summer Big Horn wind. Red ghosts shouldered into the lower surrounding hillocks, around to the east where the country slid off toward the Rosebud, around to the west above the waters of the Little Big Horn, around to the south to nowhere, and to the north where the amber ghost of yellow hair straddled its final coulee. Sitting Bull, somewhere, folded his hands. Crazy Horse mounted. Cheyenne children dipped water out of the river and watched warily up the waterless ridge.

It was as silent as the bottom of an ancient sea. The conscience, soundless, irreducibly colorless, of humankind rode in upon the winds of chance. A novel, a fantasy to be sure, took form in my brain, where the silver and coal and grass rose up against human malefaction and smote it forever down.

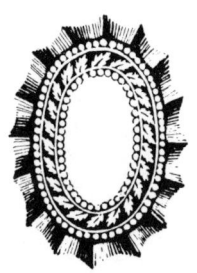

IV. Grass

We crossed into Sheridan County, Wyoming, on a moonless night of stars and bad road. This was the country of *The Grassman*, and the bookselling pitch was about to narrow, thematically, at least until we had trekked southward to Wyoming's metropolitan city of Casper. One more county down was Johnson, and one east, Campbell, where the grassplains roll out toward Dakota in an endless, flattening series of dry creeks and prehistoric distances. It is called, this sweep of earth, the Thunder Basin National Grasslands, and it is being riddled for its oil and coal by dark metallic modern monsters that from a distance look like the dinosaurs that once lived here. I had walked and driven it, sat in the torrent of July heat to stare at the shortgrass, the sunflowers, and the shimmering silhouette of the Pumpkin Buttes. It was a kind of coming back, this trip, for it had been more than a dozen years since I'd sought to amalgamate the psychogeographic possibilities of this purest of all Western land, with the mythic blood-curse of the *Oresteia*. What had taken my interest in the very seminal moment of understanding something of the Aeschylian notion of morality and tragedy, was the effect of *place* on those larger, archetypal cycles—not so much specific place, either, but place as one of life's (and myth's) inescapables. That amalgam had worked out across a quite American theme, and now it rode glued to the backside of my soul down the east edge of the Horn.

Carol Berge once said of writing erotica for her magazine, *Center:* "Whatever you do, make it Olympian." That should be said also if you choose to coat your notions, however mythic, tragic, or psychoblahblah, with Western theme and content. As I looked toward the great Big Horns on the west and the Nine Mile Hills on the east I wondered, perhaps for the first real time, whether I'd gotten the size of it all into this novel. Somehow I knew the land knew. And somehow I knew that this place had been flogged enough with bad Zane Grey.

The Grassman had been researched and written a dozen years earlier. In the intervening time its dialogue and descriptive prose had been cut and reworked, but the basic story with its forty or fifty characters had been a project of some other time for me, some other place, temperament and obsession. Alan Swallow was the first publisher to see it, had possession of it in fact when he died in 1966. After some difficulty in retrieving it from the new Swallow org in Chicago, I allowed it to lie dormant except for spasms of rewriting. In December of 1967 I got inebriated with Curt Gentry [*The Last Days of the Late Great State of California*] one night in San Francisco and let the fact of the manuscript's existence slip to him. "I'm going to tell my publishers about you," he said liquidly, and we laughed. But in three days I'd received letters from those publishers—proof of the superiority of Gentry's memory over the sauce, and of the squeeze he had then with New York. (Also of his comparative ignorance of the size, complexity and general unpublishability of the book.) Shortly thereafter I consummated my divorce from big publishing via a long, cordial correspondence with a Norton editor. The manuscript lay again dormant, except for the spasms, until Thorp Springs Press brought it out in June, '74.

So that I related to it now more as a salesman than an author. It gave, I think, an advantage, a merciful sort of objectivity in confronting the marketeers. If there was anything in my carrying case I felt defensive about it was that *Whole COSMEP Catalog*—which created such a blue bolt of expectation! But the lesson for the entire trip grew clear to me in this bleak and beautiful high plainsland: do not linger in ego-pain or you will be left as mercantile carrion. Move on. Anything that helps objectify the task is good. And, as Berge said, keep it Olympian whatever you do.

In all of Johnson County, then, there is only one stash of the book. That is in Buffalo, where we visited the local library and museum, and where I talked with the young librarian who said the coal or oil or both were about to boom the place. Later we saw the effects of oil in the town of Gillette, which has been concentrically ringed with mobile homes, and whose streets are overloaded circuits close to fire. It was a terrifying nightmare from the '50's: 12:00 midnight and streams of cars careened along a prefabbed Main Street. It was a flood tide and, once caught, it was impossible to stop, brake, hard even to turn out of the press and crush. We were figures in a pinball machine and a sadist kept feeding it dimes.

From Buffalo it is more than 100 miles south to Casper, Wyoming's metro center. You pass through the town of Midwest, site of one of the world's largest light oil producing fields, It is perhaps the most inhospitable place in the state, with every rise and gully for a half-dozen square miles around the Salt Creek spotted with slowly-grinding black oil rigs. The town itself is prefabricated, its dirt streets lined with houses, one exactly the same as the next (the oilman's imagination, no doubt), and each lot marked off with strands of lead piping in lieu of fence. It offends the nose and eye and heart, and the great trucks of commerce offend the ear. South another five miles is the infamous Teapot Dome, source of the oil scandal in the 1922 Harding administration.

In Casper we had forty minutes to hit three stores and one newspaper during the 4:30 traffic rush, and made it with about five minutes to spare. We placed books in all three stores, got a promise of a review from a young newspaperman named Joe Wheelan of the Casper Star Tribune. "They give me jobs no one else will do," he told me, and we grinned, he and I, knowing more than all the rest of them put together.

Back north again we slipped along the upper edge of the Grasslands into Campbell County. You circle the Pumpkin Buttes this way, and move up the Belle Fourche, which drains itself into Thunder Basin. Ellen worked the camera and I wrote down names of likely locations—be Olympian, we thought, come back in a year, two, maybe five—they can't rape it that fast, or can they?—and make the movie. *You can't do it,* I thought. *You can't get this into a can—or a novel either for that matter.* It defies capture.

The sun slid behind the Buttes in the lowering haze. The great trucks that had blasted the quiet air earlier had ceased. We passed a ewe and her lamb on the road, both dead from civilization. A band of horses played grabass to our right near the Belle Fourche crossing.

Stylish devils! Free as a windsong! How much of this basin you seen?!

That night we made Sundance.

New York was two thousand miles.

V. Winds and Walls

New York was two thousand miles, yah! And whether you like it or not that is just about the cast of its orbit. If New York figures into your mission in any way, you will feel its psychic gravity in Spearfish or Sturgis, and the dry winds that haunt Dakotah summers crowd your guts and your baggage downland toward ironwheeled commerce. New York is the sucking-lips of the great distended American belly, and its inhalation is aimed west for anything it can get. You feel it, Saint Gawd. You drop into the current and set sail for the home port of the demon-god ships of American Enterprise.

But we abided some with civilized country first. Like Spearfish, Belle Fourche, Sturgis. Spearfish was tourists, and two bookplaces no bigger than a fly's ass, but receptive, cordial, and in the mood for small-time trade. The existence there of the Black Hills State College helped, a small and very lush little place on a dryland bluff overlooking town. There was some summer student action, but we inkled, finally, that tourism was the main vogue at this point in the season, and so pushed north to Belle Fourche (pop. 4,200) where five main highways converged. A fact to keep in mind bookselling in tourist areas is that most merchants plan and order during the *non*-tourist season, which on the northwestern plains is winter. Therefore, when you land amongst them in mid-season at tourist-time you find them overworked, out-of-sorts if it's not going well, and disinclined to increase inventories. You have to suggest that your books are not *necessarily* souvenirs, but also good winter company for the locals—and if the merchant *closes* in the winter, forget it and send brochures when the snow flies. I think much of the material produced by small presses could sell well in these areas—but you should see to getting paid, too, before cold shuts down the telegraph wires.

Belle Fourche (Bal-Foosh) claimed to be the geographic center of the U.S. (count Alaska and Hawaii) and teemed with everything but books. We combed the town twice, not even finding an NAL rack in a supermarket. In a kind of reactive flinch we scouted the four or five booteries in a vain attempt to replace my rough-out riding boots that collapsed in Oregon (as the Apache leathers I'd worn since then were now collapsing) but found only forty-dollar spats, spangled enough to scare hell out of the meanest horse west of the Missouri.

"Boots've gone to the square-dancers," I grumbled to a young clerk.

"Really," he grinned, and I knew that that goddamned adverb-becoming-expletive had slithered into the heartland lingo too. I thought of a play—maybe Richard Morris would write it—composed of two characters and one word—*really*—with all manner of intonations. But then there was that Dakotah sun, and we moved southeast.

Sturgis sits out of protection from the Black Hills; it is treeless country, simply ransacked by the red-hot winds that chew into western South Dakota. We found one store here that carried books, and I spent far more time and energy than good sense trying to get the woman proprietor to venture $3.54 on two *Grassman*s. Her final remark was that they'd just have to get the book somewheres else. At a gas station about four rods down the avenue a rotund man with hypertrophied shoulders glad-handed me and my empty tank. He seemed high on his own misery, talked like a fine-tuned set of in-line pistons (and listnened about as well), complained about Means and Banks while he shoveled ten bucks of fuel at me.

"They're just like white men," he said, hitching his britches and snaking the ten out of my hand. "They're as bad as any white man. See ya." And he was gone as he'd come, talking. I flopped back into the car.

"What was that all about?" Ellen asked.

"Christ I'm not sure. But I think we've about run out the string here in Sturgis."

We ducked back into the Black Hills at Deadwood, where Jack McCall shot Hickock, and where Calamity Jane lies buried next to Sam Bass. Between there and Mount Rushmore to the south, down Dakota 385, rides the main heft of the Black Hills tourist traffic. The treed hills loop in overhead in a storm of dense, rugged beauty. Deadwood itself was jammed and hot, and after a futile attempt to turn up the manager of the Dry Gulch Art Gallery, we swung across to the twin city of Lead.

While Deadwood thrives unabashedly on bars, gimmicks and two or three historical shootings, Lead (leed) remains (or so it smells) an authentic mining town. It is a tunnel through the high, close red-black buildings which ooze unkempt age and recalcitrance.

"Between here and back in Deadwood there *has* to be a bookstore." I mumbled as we drove up the narrow main street incline. Like Butte in Montana, Lead pushes the mind backward a century. It has that shadowed, shoddy reality. We spotted a Chamber of Commerce, and Ellen inquired within. Only Western Drug, they said. But, as moments later I stood amidst the perfumes and lotions, I realized the Chamber was out of touch and date. There were no books. I threw *The Grassman* up anyway.

"How much discount?"
"Forty percent."
"I'll try one."
"Paperback or hardback?"
"Oh, one of each."

The Chamber was now up-dated, and even today I wonder how and where those books got displayed.

Down 385 is Rushmore, a sculptural Hydra whacked and blasted into a great, sheer face of solid rock, four heads of Great White Fathers stamped forever, like a brand, into the Indian's most cherished earth. I thought of Sturgis: *They're as bad as any white man.* And I had this sense of Means and Banks, chisels, ropes, dynamite, scaling the sheer wall of Arrogance behind Rushmore and smacking away.

Bookstores are among the most fleeting of retail commerce. The yellow pages are never reliable, and you need to case the main arteries of each city with a roving eye and a hopeful heart. Look for the oo's. Ellen got so sharp at this that we were yanking into toolsheds, bootstores and good-anythings. It paid off many times, twice in Rapid City with the Pauper's Bookstore, a new, general outlet, and the Clearing House (for mind and media) run by a good person named John, who could not afford to buy anything but who made good talk.

Fifty miles east of Rapid City is another white phenomenon that matches Rushmore shred for shred and lump for lump. It is known as Wall Drug, a rambling, compartmented marketplace that straddles the dusty town of Wall (pop. 786). On the grass-plains from every direction for hundreds of miles there are signs assuring you that Wall Drug is just ahead. The signs themselves, it is boasted, are so notable (and noticeable) that every state has them somewhere, and even some foreign countries. The whole program started in the early part of the century when an enterprising young couple decided to advertise "free icewater" at their pharmacy. It's a circus, as American-white as wooden Indians. Wall Drug encloses at least one bookstore, with racks of paperbacks elsewhere. The store seems to contain the newest popular material, and much western Americana, both fiction and non-fiction. There seemed to me to be room for something fresh, different. Somehow the place exuded that possibility. When I finally tracked down the manager through the wash of shoppers he was so harried that I got five words: *see us in the winter.* Madness.

The town of Wall acquired its name, apparently, because it sits north of a long escarpment known as the Bad Lands Wall, "wall" being a term in the West for this particular land feature of wind erosions. In the higher West the walls tend to have a homogenous reddish cast; in the Badlands, maybe six hundred square miles of one precipitous vestige upon another, the rock strata are lighter and exquisitely beautiful. Each mile unfolds a new vestige and a new rainbow of pastel colors. The Badlands are not old, geologically, and the steady winds enlarge them at a vigorous rate.

South, I knew from the map, lay Wounded Knee, one item only in a monstrous epoch, yet itself containing enough history to stun the mind and soul. The names were familiar all the way down: Potato Creek, Porcupine, Manderson, Pine Ridge. We didn't go. One more pair of white in-riders with no answers was not needed. The chasm in timespirit dwarfs the one of space from Wall Drug to Wounded Knee. We moved east, soberly, across the Missouri River.

We learned another way of going in Sioux Falls, though the method worked better in some subsequent cities. One advantage of having a large publisher for your book is that, out of self-interest to be sure, the publisher furnishes all manner of press releases and publicity out ahead of you, so that when you arrive on a scene you are not an upstart stranger; you have credentials. I had no such "advance notice"—though I think next time I will prepare that myself and litter the prospective trail ahead with it as much as possible. The second best thing is to visit the local media first, especially the local dailies in small cities. You present the book, try to get a commitment to review, and find out the name of the possible reviewer. This allows you to speak with some local knowledge to booksellers, *all* of whom are conscious of newspaper bookspace. At least one later reviewer opened his piece with a rap about that technique itself.

In Sioux Falls, the Argus-Leader promised some space, and that helped sell books for us at Augustana College and Sioux Falls College. The area's major outlet, Dalton, gave us the old shuffle to its Minneapolis central office, and in two or three other cases managers were out or minds closed irretrievable. In a last-gasp effort to cover that town I hit the Dakota News Agency, the local magazine and paperback distributor, who took a 47% discount and consignment on fifty *Grassman*s. If the local media were the first thing to visit, the local distributor probably should be the last.

We were in the midwest—and New York's orbital force grew.

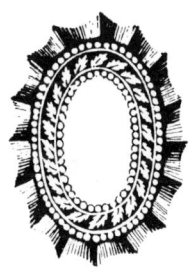

VI. East of Ninety-Eight

The Ninety-eighth Meridian slashes through the center of the country's cornbasket, entering somewhere just east of Devil's Lake in North Dakota, crossing the Missouri near Niobrara, Nebraska, through Wichita Falls, Texas, and into Mexico west of Brownsville. It is an artifice of cartographers to be sure, but: the rate of water evaporation is 30-60 inches per summer west of 98, under 35 east; rainfall is under 20 inches west, over 20 east; trees grow abundantly east of 98, but not west; wind velocity is 10-14 mph west of it, under 10 east; west there are 3 days of hail per year, east only 2; short grass grows west, tall grass east; cotton grows east, but not west. Roughly, Meridian Ninety-eight divides the Great Plains from the Prairie Plains—and the west from the midwest.

As we crossed the Mississippi into LaCrosse late one night the heat and dampness recalled an old addiction. A sign along the crossing told of an ice cream parlor just south of town. "Two states know how to eat," I said out of the Mississippi mist, and I could see Ellen—who had studied French cooking—thinking *here comes the apple pie—and maybe mom too.* "I mean *eat*, you know?" I rattled. "I mean like just *food*—no starvation in the name of culture, no ritual funnybusiness—"
"What besides Wisconsin?" she said calmly (she'd seen the sign too).
"Pennsylvania."

Books were another matter.
"But this is a land of progressive politics," I fussed next day.
"Politics is not reading. It's more eating than reading."
"This is a jock university," Peter Brunner told us. He was manager of the U-W, LaCrosse bookstore, which was a corner of the cafeteria fenced off by glass. "Nobody *reads* here." Brunner knew some small press people from Madison and Milwaukee— Mangelsdorff, Edelson, Kois. We placed some books with him and

with McKay's across the street, and felt fortunate. We rapped too long with Brunner, and made Madison (147 miles) by late afternoon, when the cement was hottest and the traffic its choking worst.

Madison held some nostalgia. It had been the site of the COSMEP Conference two years before, a good, loosely-knit meeting concocted by Morris Edelson, editor of *Quixote* these past ten years. I had come in that time on a plane early and found Morris waiting. "We have no transportation," was the way he said hello. "I'll rent a car and ferry people in," I said. (One metermaid ticketed that damned car five times before I left the city.) We stayed at the YMCA where at least the candy machines worked, and where George Mattingly and I and others sat in the dim hall on the top floor smoking late into the night. The area was called "the Third Coast" by those who felt the first two were steamrolling culture. The COSMEP women gathered their forces in Madison for the first time in '72 and began the long process of raising consciousnesses that still goes on. The COSMEP "Manual Project" was first proposed here, and Felix Pollak's library at UW, boasting the best collection of littlemags worldwide, was much visited. The COSMEP Directors added another Board member, Glenna Luschei. And on the shore of one of those lakes I talked for the last time with my friend Bill Wantling, about myth and archetype.

This time it was more frenzied. We had less than an hour to cover this huge city before the stores closed. Ellen slid into a phone booth (more an oven at that point) and I into a drug store after a map. When she emerged with a list of 15 stores I had the map already frying over-easy on the car-hood.

"This is where we are," I said, like Hood at the gates of Chickamauga.

"And this is where we're going," she answered as swiftly as George B. Thomas, pointing uproad into the snorting center of Madison. "Most of these are on State or University. State is loaded." Yankee gold. Five stores in two tight blocks.

The next hour was madness born of one-way treets, illegal parking (but no metermaid) and traffic from a surrealistic disaster movie. We made a dozen stores, left books in two—both of them on State Street, which turned out otherwise to be overrated in both my memory and the phone book: some stores had specialized into

occult, yoga, metaphysical, used, rare, etc. Others were simply cynical of folks peddling. A visit with an old mail customer, Mosely, fell victim to the busyness too, and we limped back out of the mid-city east to find the Wisconsin Independent News Department, which we'd heard was an alternative distributor. When that address proved deserted we retreated yet another league east into the East Towne Mall and fell upon Walden Books and the Zondervan Family Bookstore, neither of which took interest in our small war. In checking another phone book here we found the yellow pages for bookstores summarily ripped out, missing. we compared some notes and determined that since somewhere in Montana we'd found these pages missing in perhaps six different phonebooks—and we began to frame a psycho-profile for, and assess the sheer *will* and *meanness* of, whoever it was selling books on the road in front of us. "If we catch him..." I muttered dizzily in the heat.
"Or her."
"I'll—I'll borrow the list!"

Later that night, after grinding through the high-speed Chicago traffic and the smoke of Gary, we pulled into South Bend, Indiana. "Pennsylvania is up ahead. It will have food. Until then, forget it."

Of the seventy-odd cities we visited over the entire trip the three worst, for different reasons, were Portland, Maine, Columbus, Ohio, and South Bend. South Bend simply lacked bookselling places of any dimension or sensible order. You have a newsstand store in the unparkable center of town, and a discount shack in a chaotic shopping center over in Mishawaka, South Bend's twin city. You have a Catholic store in someone's house with almost no stock (even Catholic) and then, again over in Mishawaka, a chainstore called Bookworld which does all of its business out of a town just north across the line, Niles, Michigan. On a trip like this you begin, out of self-preservation if not practice, to develop an early "cognitive map" for a given city, so that you have a broad sense of where you are and where you're going most of the time. South Bend simply defied construction of such a map—even when we'd been lost and found in it a dozen times that next day.

Beyond the heat there was another irritant—an Airstream Trailer convention which had drawn, some said, five thousand of those little silver hot-boxes onto the Notre Dame Campus. You could spot the Airstream folks no matter where they were, cluttering the streets or the malls in a spirit of listless celebration. The landscape around ND was silver, like a harborfull of moth-balled vessels. The sun glinted off them everywhere you turned and poked at the eyes and mind through the silver-hung air. There was no entrance to the campus, no visiting the university bookstore. You risked silver-blindness on every turn. I have never seen so much of any one thing in my life.

We followed up the trail of another rumored distributor, and after some snarl found a group called The Distributor in a big, new basement warehouse—air conditioned. We studied row upon row of stock—a fine selection. Turns out most of the distribution is north and west, toward Detroit and Chicago. I recommend this distributor, especially to those small presses within a hundred or two miles of South Bend.

After Chicago and the Indiana and Ohio Turnpikes northern Pennsylvania was a geo-wonder. A gentle weather pattern harassed us as we moved through those wild, cool mountains toward New York. The pull of that city, the bookfair, meant drive, don't sell, and we sailed through the eastern green of hills not gone to coal. We didn't even stop to check the yellow pages in the towns we passed. The heart of the artichoke was so close that we could sacrifice the tender, inner leaves.

When next day we pulled into Port Jervis, where three state borders converge, we were refreshed and ready for the New York Book Fair ahead. There were no stores in Port Jervis, and not much in Middletown up the line, but I had to visit Middletown all the same. Nostalgia, I guess: in '58 I came out of New England beaten and broke, looking for a leg west. In Middletown I hooked on for ten months with a tabloid newspaper called the Middletown Daily Record, one of the first offset dailies in the country, locked in a capital suicide-struggle with another daily (the town had 25,000 people), the Times-Herald. The town's only newspaper now is called the Times-Herald-Record—which completes a capsule history of newspaper publishing in small town America.

It was raining this day, July 5, 1974. In fact the bookstore, Our Place , had sprung a leak and lost some books to it. I slipped back to the rain-winter of 1958-59, a misery throughout southern New York for sleek, rain-frozen highways, Rockefeller's first year as Governor, in fact—and my last east of Meridian Ninety-eight. I had lived in a small apartment in Circleville three miles away, and that is where the plot and story of *The Grassman* had taken rudimentary shape.

No one on the staff of the Middletown Times-Herald Record even remembered the newspaper war or anyone connected with it. Names meant nothing. *That* made me feel suddenly old—then suddenly very smug: they had not only missed the excitement, they even lacked a sense of their own history, they even lacked a curiosity for it! It had nothing to do with age—many of them were older than I. It had to do with weariness. Now it was just a business, a part of a vast corporate chain of small dailies. They sent me to the editor of the Women's Pages. She tried to be interested, between phone calls about marriages and coming-outs, but I was, simply, another book-pusher looking for space.

I slipped away during one of those phone calls, leaving a copy of the book to its fate—probably a bottom drawer. When I hit the streets it was raining harder. A mist was moving into the old city as if trying to bury it forever. Sixty miles from the world's greatest commerce, we used to say, and yet backward as they come.
I moved out of the past. Tomorrow the city.

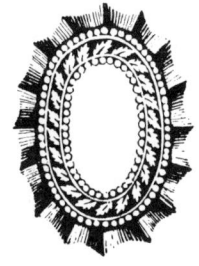

VII. Gravity's Zero

Noo Yawk. Once here, we knew what the coming had been: an increasing tension in all elastic parts, a subtle hurrying, awareness of the hostile brushing of too many bodies in a space, the fading away of that free second cup of coffee—and of the time and mood to drink it in.

In the stretch of a deepening urban landscape, watching the distances shrink between one temperament and another—one boundary, one sign and the next—we planned city-strategy. No paranoids we. I was born and raised in NYC, lived there 18 years. But age and distance tell. What do you do with a car full of books in New York? What do you do without one? We had sent eight cartons of Dustbooks stock to Jackie Eubanks, per instructions, and several more had been mailed from Berkeley with the not inconsiderable *Whole COSMEP Catalog*. What we didn't know, as per not having received instructions before we left, was how we were to get these books from Jackie's Brooklyn address to Huntington Hartford Museum/New York Cultural Center. Now, when I knew it, it had no pretensions to culture; it was the Huntington Hartford Museum. It stood on tiptoe on concrete arches that surely would one day fall under its uninteresting bulk. It was, to our high school snobberies, only slightly less ridiculous than the Schenley Building's cupric acid sunsets. But now it was New York's Cultural Center, gravity's zero that had pulled us by the front fender all the length of the continental spine.

No paranoids we, but as the land shrank we veered, tacked north to Hartford's Bradley Field, to leave the car and approach the apple in the guise of pilgrims. We called New York, discovered that Jackie had masterfully arranged the transfer of all packages to the Council on Interracial Books, but a mere two blocks from The Hunt. Perfect. The tremulous scent of faintly turning milk hovered, but only in the inconceivable distance. No, she didn't remember seeing Dustbooks packages arrive, but others had accepted packages in her absence—and would we come early, say 8:00, to help her set up?

How to go to a Bookfair without any books:

First, make sure you leave your car which contains at least some samples of your publications and your brochures, in another city, better yet, another state. Second, arrive very early, skip breakfast, so you can carry huge display tables out of storage and set them up on non-consecutive floors because the staff of The Hunt neglected to do it. Third, help cart and sort everyone else's shipment while making sure your own is not there. Fourth, rent, in addition to you own table, one for COSMEP, so you can sell the *Whole COSMEP Catalog*. Fifth, stir and enjoy with no smoking allowed from 10:00 a.m. to 10:00p.m. on three consecutive days. And by Gutenberg you will—enjoy that is. Poor but happy.

The Fair was a howler. There was too little space, behind tables, in front of tables; too few elevators that moved too slowly; too little time to talk to people who stopped at the table; no time to see the rest of the fair. There was insufficient of everything except people. They came in droves, and drove, and came (George Plimpton pedaled). The second day rumors—you could hear them pass from table to table with the hush of a first night hit—"They're lined up around the block." And they were. The guards, yes, I mean that, were admitting them only 12 at a time because of the fire laws, don't you know. (We set off an alarm by mistakenly opening a fire door, and no one seemed to care.) In the Big Apple they came, from the granite-spined central city, the blase-capital of the world. The puzzled and curious: "Who the hell are you people? What's a small press?" The disaffected: "My friend had a book published by a major publisher and they remaindered it six months later." Friends: "I want the new Directory. Whaddya mean you don't have any copies? Take an order?" We counted the money we were losing. Joe Bruchac loaned us a sample copy of the *Small Press Review* on African Presses that he had guest edited. We took orders madly for about two hours before it was ripped off. So we tied a balloon to the one copy of the Directory we had in a suitcase. At least we'd see it go. There was the satisfaction of watching *The Grassman* sell. Thorp Springs was sharing a table with our non-existent stock and we could watch the green pile shrink next door.

An old timer from Doubleday came by, who was, it turned out, also an old Dustbooks customer. John Brockman gave a cocktail party to mix big weenie editors with their alternatives. Bill Henderson sold *The Publish It Yourself Handbook* in his own town. Some ladies, yes, I mean that, from apple-based big mags signed mailing lists promising to make up for their previous inattention to small presses. Len had a telephone interview with *Seventeen*, but they declined to let him mention Shameless Hussy Press; teenage audience, dontcha know. There was T.V. coverage, the fair made page 5 of the *New York Post*, and broke a small hole in the back window (last page, Book Review) of the *New York Times*.

And we talked COSMEP. Well, we had the *Catalog*, so, of course we must know all about the COSMEP Conference which ran partly with, partly after the Bookfair. Only we didn't. We had no time to get over to Columbia, and no one gave us a schedule. So we gave directions uptown, pointed people, wrote down Richard Morris's address, made appointments to "get back to you" when we could get a schedule. Nancy Henderson finally gave us one copy, which I copied, others copied for themselves for the next two days. "COSMEP stands for the Committee of Small Magazine Editors and Publishers and Presses (Thanks, Frederick Morey)..." until by Wednesday I had all the voice of a 12-year-old at camp on the day after Junior Olympics. Didn't eat much, though I found stale danish especially plentiful in the Columbus Circle area, and Foster Roberston reported a nice Indian restaurant in walking distance. Didn't sleep much either; all of New York was left for after 10:00 p.m.

And when the show folded, we struck our tables (we got one hour to wipe all traces of ourselves from Huntington's House forever), made impossible arrangements through impossible traffic with a car commandeered from a good-humored Joe Ribar and Lyn Lifshin, got the rest of the *Catalogs* into temporary storage with Harry Smith. We had, then, some money, a mailing list of librarians, cynics, readers, the curious, the eccentric, the arcane; we had elation, laryngitis; we had—a conference to attend.

The COSMEP Conference carried much of the Bookfair momentum, even with its concomitant exhaustion, into dorms and on to the panels. The vitality of success (a little dab'll do ya) made issues—distribution, the *Whole COSMEP Catalog*, The Challenge of the Small Presses—seem pressing matters again, still. I liked the interchange of the Women's meetings, though I still couldn't speak above a whisper and did more "inter"ing than changing. Listened and listened to the French women from Editions des Femmes who flew from Paris to sell their books on the street in front of The Hunt, then stayed for the conference. And, in a self indulgent moment, I took an afternoon to visit a friend in yes Bedford Stuyvesant, yes alone, yes returning after dark, yes alone, in a paint-bombed mosaic of an IRT subway. And I saw the city again.

I had lived in New York for years, and I talked about books to friends, but I never before saw New York through the double-o glasses of books. The Bookfair, the Conference simply transformed the city by placing it exclusively in relation to books, transformed its people into readers. Paul Foreman and Len sold copies of *The Grassman* to people waiting in line for an uptown movie, while we, too, waited in that line, and signed and sold enough copies to pay for our tickets. Ina Wilde's guide to eating cheap and healthy in New York guided us finely to food, over which we talked about books: spaghetti with Anne Pride and Hugh Fox and Geoff Sills; packaged cookies and coke in the Columbia Quad with Jack Frazier, Anne; a lemony chicken with olives, and my first meeting with Fred Morey. Bookstores jumped at us from between drugstores and bars, just walking to dinner. New York *is* a kind of Big Apple, fight it though we may, and its relation to books is intimate, even when destructive, restrictive and hostile. It's not that we polished it, or put it in a Christmas stocking. But what the bookfair did, what the conference did, was give us a bite. And for the moment we forgot that it was overripe from heat and crowding, mealy with interbreeding, getting soft. Because the bite was sweet, and the taste lingered.

We flew out to Hartford like Willy Loman, heading for the New England territory.

VIII. Green Skies

From its icewater coast to its dense, deciduous hills, New England is a jut of hard American hide left geographically on its own hook in the North Atlantic. A great white whale still plumbs the seas of its conscience, and the certain slanted light of its afternoon holds still the shadows of Hawthorne, Longfellow and Thoreau. There remains a bleakness here for me, however more fixed in past than present, that oppresses like a winter Sunday. For all the years I knew him, and many before, my father, a Canadian Scot, rassled this grey horned ethic from the Merrimack mill towns to Gloucester on the sea, and far away along the mud-banks of the LaMoille River in northern Vermont. It never made just return to him for his long labors, I always thought, yet to his last day, a bow in his hand, he cherished that hard ground and rooted himself to it. I took the road, it turns out, for both of us.

"Somewhere within a hundred miles," I said to Ellen as we pushed north from Hartford, "I would have to say was home."

"I, too." She looked back toward the New York City we'd just left.

Ah, that was the northeast I knew! You were always within a hundred miles of everything! I recalled a Californian reading my novel *Dark Other Adam Dreaming* in manuscript and commenting that I insisted (oddly) on three miles being such a long way. In California you drive a hundred miles to work; in northern New England in the late forties (the novel's period) you fought each mile of mud-road for a share of your psychesoul.

I had worked here once in northern Connecticut for a tobaccoman, hanging the stalks, six to a lathboard, in long airless rows high up in dusty tobacco sheds. Sometimes we were forty feet above the dirt floor, and the beams we stood on were loose and rolled from underfoot. *What if we fall?* I had wondered to the man working next to me. *You'll grab something before you go too far*, he said with grit on his teeth. It beat cutting the stuff in the fields, which was where I'd started.

We cut a great loop through New England, as if to run backwards through a life that now belonged, for me, in a novel that a year hence (and with a little luck) might scandalize the place. Westfield's one viable bookstore took on copies of *The Grassman*. "My mother will sell them if nothing else," I pointed out. I talked with the proprietor about small press publishing and he grew interested, decided to stock the Directory. Over at the *News Advertiser*, where I'd done my last gig in the region in '58, it was business as usual. A home-town boy you say? Well, leave the book. It was here, fifteen years ago now, that I stood in the town square and watched a young Senator Kennedy come into town in a two-car motorcade. A real estate man I knew introduced Kennedy as "the next President." His partners gave him hell for that afterwards. But it was Jackie's wrinkled skirt that somehow stuck in my memory.

That night in the town of Agawam ten miles away I gave a talk on small press publishing in the local library. The people of Agawam packed the place with body and spirit, and held me long with their interest and kindness. Here was something, I thought, to controvert the seeming melancholia this land brought to me!

In Springfield next day the street struggle reconstituted itself as tooth-and-nail we moved books into three stores at city center and squeezed a promise of review out of Wayne Phaneuff on the *Daily News*. Phaneuff, it turns out, was more interested in California and the West than in my local origins, and I kept that in mind as we pushed deeper into old haunts. In Manchester, New Hampshire, I visited with Joe McQuade of the *Union Leader*, whose oft-infamous publisher William Loeb had given him a book to review. McQuade dug it out of a drawer and showed it to me. "Do you know who this guy is?" Indeed I did! He was a crazy preacher (whose name now escapes) whom I'd many times seen shouting his wares on the Sproul Plaza in Berkeley. Loeb, it seems, has a fascination for the odd while expatiating hard, rightwing causes. Of all the newspapers I visited the *Union Leader* had the toughest security check, though the Omaha *World Herald* ran it a close second, and the *New York Times* has a small army of thugs stationed at its entrance.

Manchester is a dim milltown straddling the Merrimack River, which originates in central New Hampshire, runs south into

Massachusetts where it turns abruptly northeast to come into the sea around Newburyport. My grandmother's brother, whom they called "the big Indian of the Merrimack," used to run it via canoe, but like many rivers it invited human intervention because it contemptuously flooded out those old milltowns come each spring. One such town, Lowell, Massachusetts where I was born (as was Kerouac) was damned near converted into mudplain in '36; they say my sisters and I were carried across a bridge over the river as waters licked its underpinnings and the span shuddered. My grandfather refused to leave, ended up on the roof in a fight for his life.

At three points in my life I lived in Manchester, the last to finish high school and put in a year and a half in a bedding factory on Lincoln Street where I learned upholstery and Canadian-American French. It seemed strange to be selling books there, but on the other hand we'd been at it for over four thousand miles and I took to the offensive with ease and objectivity. Two downtown stores stocked the novel, but the city had clearly given way to peripheral shopping malls, and so we made our way to Bedford where such a mall existed. We left eleven *Grassman*s scattered throughout the Manchester area; and months later I learned that an old friend of mine upon hearing of the book went out and bought up every copy he could find (six). If I went back to Manchester right now I could sell more books—but damned if they'll order by mail. There you have the dilemma. By my arithmetic you increase your chances by a factor of forty with a personal visit—something the encyclopaedia publishers have known all along.

We crossed at Kittery and moved deliberately up through seventy miles of Maine's seacoast "vacationland". The names broke in on me like the saltwind: York Beach, Ogunquit, Wells, Kennebunkport, Goose Rocks Beach, Old Orchard, Biddeford-Saco—it was a gauntlet I'd run many times with my old friend Bob Fay and a summer newspaper we called the *Tourist Topic* (A Summer Guide to Maine's Southern Seacoast Splendor"). *It may still be going*, I thought as we slipped into Kennebunkport where Bob and I had kept our office. I tried to find that office to prove that the entire thing had happened, but the building had vanished. The need to authenticate the past grew: "I remember the day Kenneth Roberts died. He lived up towards Goose Rocks there, had an interest in water dowsing, wrote a book called *The Seventh Sense.*" Twenty years is long. "Met Cameron Mitchell in a restaurant right over there." The restaurant had vanished. I remembered the printing bills that had mounted against "The Topic" until at last a newspaper publisher from Lewiston up the way owned it all.

A water channel cuts the quaint town asunder and we ate at a place built over that channel. About a lobster-throw away, across the tiny square, I visited with the local bookseller and lost a scrap to mogul publishing by coming on too fast. He was not interested in small press information if that information was not in the standard trade volumes. "They have everything I want," he said, and waved me off. If you must challenge, I learned again, do it slowly, gently.

If I'd had the money I would have bought an Arentz seascape, partly because of sentiment, mostly because Arentz was the greatest seascape artist I ever saw. I found some of his grand oils once as far away as Denver, and recklessly wondered how it would be if he'd been turned loose in the high West.

Heaven and Hell are literary extravaganzas. They are a way of arranging your character personas along several dimensions in literary form—in time, in morality, in place, etc. If my own persona belonged to a literary character, for instance, Heaven along the *place* dimension might be Bozeman, or Thunder Basin. Certainly Hell along that same dimension would be the city of Portland, Maine!

For Portland is the plain meanest town I know, bearing on the absolute front edge of Yankee recalcitrance and visionlessness. I lived in its center for almost two years in a fifth-floor tenement, held more odd jobs than I can count in an effort to squeeze through two years of college, and saw every frailty I possessed magnified in a long, unaltering string of ill-luck. Portland is greying red brick; poverty punished by wintry sleet straight off the awesome Atlantic; it is gaunt factories that were collapsing in '55 when I got there and are now a sort of rubble, nineteen years later; it is the lost "r" in the twanging speech which manifests a lost adventure somewhere in the soul; it is sea-based oil paraphernalia jammed into its waterways, and oil-stink mixed with salt air and tar; it is weathered lobstermen with hands the breadth of a paddle who lean against the pulverizing tide; it is a peninsula with no place to go, so keeps stirring its crumbling ingredients into a vat of Longfellow stew. Ten miles off in any direction Maine is a beautiful land—but Portland festers.

And now, too, it was futile and agonizing. I planted some bio-data with the *Press Herald*, which promised a story, but that information was useless on deaf ears. One storeman was an honest John: "This town doesn't *read*," he said. "Look, I do a hundred a week out front here—and a thousand a week out back." I looked in the back. It was porn. "Tough place," I said, and he grinned. Jones' Bookstore, less than two blocks from where I'd lived, would not take *The Grassman* because its blurb said the author "felt uncomfortable east of the Mississippi." The cycle of madness fed upon itself once more. The *Maine Sunday Telegram* later ran a review titled "Journalist with a Sixgun" and I meanly hoped for the worst for Portland booksellers. ·

"I've *got* to leave some books in this goddamned town," I bleated to the young bookstore proprietor at the University of Maine. "And you're my last hope. You're also my Alma Mater." The place had changed so since I'd spent two years in study there that I could not locate myself. But the intellectual experience was a as fresh as ever, washing as it had the U.S. Army out of my guts. A man named John Jaques had trusted my brain to hold more than anyone had before.

The young proprietor took a mitful of books, but it was only to be a brief break in the weather. When I returned to California a few weeks later the books were waiting marked "refused".

Portland possesses a bright spot for the small presses, however. It is a jobber called Eastern Book Company down on Middle Street along the edge of the red rubble. Like Baker & Taylor (and once Richard Abel), Eastern Book sells mainly to libraries and institutions. I visited with Dan McDonough there, looked over the vast stock of books, and left with the notion that if Eastern Book is all there is here, it is probably enough.

Later that day we sold books up the coast in Falmouth, and moved on into Freeport, home of L.L. Bean—and yet another of my late-fifties haunts. My friend Bob and I had abandoned the Kennebunkport office once the tourist summer was over down on the coast, and had come to a small letterpress newspaper plant here, he to run a paper called the Lisbon Enterprise, I one called the Freeport Press. They were tiny, bootstrap weeklies with circulations of a thousand or so, and in perhaps too young and swift an instant we killed them both and replaced them with one big tabloid called The Weekly News. We fought ignorance, our own mostly, and one brutal snowstorm upon the other until by spring we were looking for any high, warm ground that life could give. I thought briefly that old Mister Bean might save us, with a full page ad a week and some endorsement, but he was a Yankee trader who dealt in hard goods, and did not chase another's fate up the icy alleys of chance.

Bean's of course, when Ellen and I pulled into Freeport, was flourishing with cars from as far away as British Columbia in the parking lot. The cold quonset hut where we'd printed those miserable weeklies was mercifully gone, like the Kennebunkport office. Maine and I had scrubbed each clean of the other!

For awhile an awful silence stormed my heart. Ellen read aloud from Curt Johnson's novel *Nobody's Perfect* (whose title I swear I suggested to him in a letter in 1969) and the comical, outrageous Mr. Schoenebatic and his friends gradually raised the spirit of this bookjourney back to its old, high plain. Ellen, to defend her ground here a moment, does not share my achromatic sentience of New England Territory. "It is the only place I know," she says, "where the trees grow a canopy over the roads so that the sky is green. When I see New England I see green."

For a spell we rode that green highway across New England's northern reaches. Some of the names were unlikely—Lisbon, Paris, Norway, Berlin—but some were apple pie: Gorham, Randolph, Lancaster, Danville—where (she's right) the sky *is* green, and the close-fitting hills are studded with white pine, hemlock, maple, and punctuated white with those incredible birches that cluster in small blizzards for mile upon mile. You drive with care for the old road twists and the mind entangles itself into the snake-tight thickets, follows up the gorges and breaks free along the top of the wind.

We crossed the Connecticut and came down into the Green Mountains in a driving rain. At the Moose, the Passumpsic and the Winooski the storm's electricity had locked itself to the water to make a midnight show of unarguable dominion. It broke along our front as we came, and it cracked down our backtrail as we went—and we took care to know just how water and greenness came to this land. Next day in Montpelier it was still raining. We sold books at the Bear Pond, a nice and unexpected find, and tracked the Winooski to Burlington.

I first came to this northcountry in 1947 when my father uprooted us from a rather suburban life in Sudbury, Massachusetts. He would be a farmer, he thought, and beat the coming recession. It was a boyhood dream to him, born of the smoke and grime of the milltowns. The farm had a hundred cows, a 1600-bucket sugarbush, and what seemed to me then to be an endlessly isolated wilderness. In an instant, or almost, I was transformed from suburban to primitive, from slouch to worker. And when, three or four years later, we lost the place to economic vagaries, I did not know how to deposit money in a city bank—but I could drive a team, operate a dump rake without sliding into its teeth, boil sap to syrup, put manure to a winter field, and survive the damndest snowstorm the north could deliver.

That northcountry is gone now, of course. The great highway we rode up to Burlington told much of it, for it slammed across the hills like a new, straight tyne with no accord to the land's true and wrinkled face. The old roads, now untravelled which I could see below and far away were losing their crumbling surfaces to history, a history of psychic seasons of work; of a pleasure-pain principle that announced itself as fast and as true as the taste of fresh fall blackberries—or chokecherries; of tools that were as vital a part of life as food—the side-rake, tedder, pung, front-pan, pulsator, hayfork (not a pitchfork), stone bolt, eveners, trace-chains, peevee and so on; of horses weighing 1800 pounds, shod to walk on ice; of weathered old barns in full function, topless silos, houses with tiny upper windows tucked under the eaves; and of cow dung plastered along those serpentine roads marking them off in time forever from the smooth and faceless highway we now traversed.

In the late forties Burlington was a cow-town where you went to get your teeth fixed or buy farm equipment or sell milk. Now it was international. You could get Greek food on Church Street. You could see cars on the UVM campus from anywhere in the universe. The town too tried to emphasize a kind of quaintness, not unlike in fact the rest of the state, which was seeing its rather ordinary old qualities achieve a worth on the New York auction blocks. I had to forgive myself for the notion that much of it all was skin-deep—like the master highways that carved Vermont into saleable quarters.

At the Burlington Free Press I visited with Barbara Vonbruns who promised a short mention (she came through within a month, too). We then ran into coffee breaks and forenoon absenteeism of every imaginable sort until we finally gave up and dropped into a restaurant ourselves to wait them out. While waiting for service, Ellen decided to try for more addresses from a phonebook, and was instructed that there was a public telephone in the back. After two cups of coffee I grew itchy after her whereabouts and arose to investigate, but just then she returned, full of fluster and hate. To get to the telephone she'd had to climb across a piano, then through a clothes rack with fifteen jackets on it—then there was no light.
"How'd you see?"
She looked incredulous. "There was a *candle* going in back of all that!"

At the Little Professor Book Center a poet named Tinker Green was the manager. He took one look at the Directory and asked if I was "with Dustbooks or something." He'd used the Directory for years—and needless to say that saved me some words! What was important there, though, was why Green had not thought to stock the Directory before my visit—underscoring once again the importance of personal contact.

The University of Vermont Bookstore also took some Directories, and we left about a dozen Grassmans in Burlington on the basis of the promised Vonbruns review. We then drove northeast through Essex, Essex Junction, Jericho, Underhill, Cambridge Junction and into Jeffersonville, where I deposited a copy of the novel in the public library, a one-roomer centrally heated with a pot-bellied wood stove. The librarian, it turned out, lived on a section of what had been my father's farm.

"That was the one gap in the history of that land we couldn't fill," she said, and seemed to want me to stay and talk longer. But I had some gaps of myself to fill, and spent the rest of the daylight reviewing landmarks and reconstructing events now a quarter of a century old. Ellen, who has been working with me editing the novel about this place, *Dark Other Adam Dreaming*, was beautifully patient with my insistence on remembering. Finally, as the rain slowed and the light began to fade we slipped up through Smuggler's Notch and wound down into Stowe, a ski-town of moneyed quaintness. Even in the forties it had been so, with the great mountain, Mansfield, standing behind it, dividing the wealthy skiers in the south from the struggling farmers in the north.

The next day, after getting lost on a dirt road trying to find Bellows Falls, we drove back into New Hampshire, sold books in Keene, and visited an old Wyoming friend who now teaches at Franklin Pierce College in Rindge. About half way down from Keene to Rindge lies a mountain called Monadnock, jutting about three thousand feet into the southern New Hampshire sky. During the '38 hurricane I lived at the foot of that mountain.

Then we turned west again, driving out of the past.

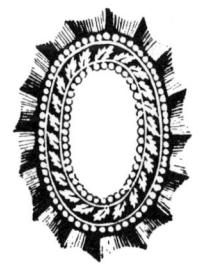

IX. Discounts and Dimes

In late summer, 1973, Dustbooks published two damned fine non-fiction books, *Conjuring A Counter-Culture* by Walt Shepperd, and *The Poetry of Pop* by Joseph Bruchac. Shepperd is the former publisher of Nickel Review, a great "pulp art" underground paper out of Syracuse, and his book contains a series of pieces he wrote before his paper's decimation by political forces at the tag-end of the sixties. Bruchac is a poet, part Native American, editor of the Greenfield Review, and "POP" (as we call it) is a careful, clear study of the lyrics of popular music as poetry. Both Shepperd and Bruchac teach in New York State Prisons, and have an empathy and rapport with prisoners that must go unmatched across the country.

They are close, long-time friends of ours, and when Ellen and I arrived in Syracuse, driving west again, they were there to see what they could do to press forward the cause of bookdom. We decided on a street sale outside the Syracuse Book Center on Marshall Street, an area akin to Berkeley's Telegraph Avenue, or High Street in Columbus, i.e., it carried the bulk of the student foot traffic and was lined with shops. We put our three books up for sale on a table along with some other material, lured customers with free potato chips and, dodging rain, sold enough to finance a party at Shepperd's place that night. The party was a true high, ending with a reading in which local writers like Ron Welburn calmed the raging rainstorm outside. Shepperd read a poem on the SLA; I read Wantling's "Earth, Ocean, Sky, History."

We spent two great days in Syracuse and visited most of the bookstores. It is a big, busy town, scattered, and we abided some with turmoil working the one-way streets and looping back to where we'd started. In the University area the Syracuse Book Center is the only likely outlet for small press titles, and downtown if you get a chance to visit with Jerry Brock, the buyer at the Economy Bookstore on South Salina, that is your best bet there. Otherwise this upstate snowbelt town can be as street-bleak as an Ontario icestorm.

The University Store itself was maddening to find and maddening once found. The young paperback buyer, standing before several cases of Jacqueline Suzanne's *Once Is Not Enough*, claimed no interest in small press information, though she would like two Directories at 40%. We had just been lost in the catacombs of the massive Student Union; it was early without coffee; parking had been no cakewalk either. Hence, in the face of recalcitrance based on what seemed a certain unnecessary adversity, I held to the "official" discount schedule (25% on 2-5 copies). When the buyer too held for her way I suggested she was better off selling Suzanne—and I walked out. It was one of those small blows you strike on a lean morning, and later the grip of its utter smallness wrinkles your brow. Yet you would do it again—and you *should* do it again, for every system needs to catharct from time to time. In twenty five dozen stores I stomped out maybe six times, which means that in every fifty stores you'll need to make a move like that for your health. For the first two or three times guilt marched with me, but I began to see that every few miles there was a windlike freedom in going while others stayed.

In fact to balance psychic tensions on a trip like this you should probably manage to stomp out once for each time you get summarily *asked* to leave.

I remembered Buffalo from 1970 when my friend Allen DeLoach, editor of *Intrepid*, organized the conference that year of the Committee of Small Magazine Editors and Publishers. I remembered it, I should say, psycho-geographically more than physio-geographically, for by the time we had run the New York Thruway from Syracuse the time was closing up our options and the weather was threatening to seal them forever. Somehow we threaded our way to a great pyramid-like center-city mall, from there the better, we figured, to plot the city bookstores, ground zero (again) as it were. But we became entombed in that mall for over an hour, searching first for a bathroom and second for a map. The bathrooms, it turned out, were all in restaurants, and these required a dime to get through the door. My options on this matter had disappeared entirely, and I spent the dime; Ellen refused flatly, grumbling something about it was *their* carpet, and continuing the maphunt. During the hunt she collided with a man who was also looking for a map, and by some *deux ex machina* they found the item and we cracked free of the pyramid.

On the street moments later we passed a lawman huddled into a crevice, staring skyward with his gun drawn. We thought (for after that mall anything was right) we'd stumbled into the middle of a local city duel-off, but shortly heard a steel door slam and turned to see a Brinks truck unloading.

"Let's sell some books and git."

William Malia, the paperback buyer at Ulbrich's, a big departmented bookstore in the middle of town, asked me what influences had played on the writing of *The Grassman*. I told him Manfred, Clark, Wister, Doby, and he took twenty five books, the largest sale of the novel directly to a bookstore in the entire trip. Naturally you can see how I was moved to bring those magical western names up again in other stores! (When Manfred later wrote to me that *The Grassman* had been written with "ink dipped from the waters of the Crazy Woman Creek" I thought first of Malia, and wanted him somehow to know he'd bought right.) Influences are important, though only the shrewdest of bookbuyers will ask after them (and only those interested in the substance of a book beyond its commercial possibilities). A buyer cannot obviously *read* the book while you're standing there, nor even contend with much written critical information, assuming you have accumulated such (which I had not at that point). If you can speak of antecedents, of comparative styles, authors to whom you would acknowledge debt, it helps locate things quickly. Some bookfolks, of course, are hip to so little that such palaver is one-sided and wasteful of time and tongue. But others feast upon it, and many I met engaged me in long, interested conversation, wasteful perhaps of time, but delicious beyond knowing.

After Ulbrich's we worked our way up Main Street and left books with Everymans and the Little Professor Book Center at the University Plaza. In both places the proprietors were interested in the NYC Bookfair, just past, and in small press publishing. I was quickly aware that local small press people like Allen DeLoach had done their homework with these booksellers, and that saved both time and saliva. If there is a single more important helpmate to all small presses in general than an active *local* small press I don't know what it would be. This is where we have the corporate moguls if we can only get it together; *they* all come from one place and their appeal is almost purely mercantile. But booksellers are human members of a community, and a local small press or two in that community can humanize the whole relationship between publishing and bookselling. So when I could say I had been in Buffalo at the COSMEP Conference in 1970 (which these booksellers remembered) and that I knew the work of certain Buffalo small presses, I had a point of contact worth something.

That Buffalo conference of the Committee of Small Magazine Editors and Publishers in 70 was perhaps the largest the organization has ever had in terms of people. For one thing, the COSMEP offices were located in Buffalo that year because COSMEP's perennial Coordinator, Richard Morris, was living there at the time. For another thing Allen DeLoach, the conference director, was an absolutely tireless organizer who insisted that as much happen as could in the space of three days—and nights. For one other thing, Buffalo at that point had some well-known names in it like Fiedler, Wieners, Creeley, Barth, Ginsberg who for better or worse drew a crowd. It was the beginning of the org's third year of life, and the beginning of my third (and last, until I tried it again in '73) as its chairman. We pioneered some group workshops there which have yet to be repeated with the same verve, and we heatedly discussed whether the org should "accept government money". I remember too visiting Niagara Falls with John Pyros, Kirby Congdon and Ralph Simmons, pausing in the pounding airwash of that great river, allowing the currents of my mind to channel back through ten years of life with a woman not yet a month dead from a grinding California auto crash. That was this town's torment for me, and all the towns thereafter, and rivers and seas until the currents had worn the final, long reality into my soul.

X. Rivertown

We had been invited to visit Pittsburgh by Anne Pride, a quite incredible person, president of a women's publishing collective called KNOW which produces pamphlets and books designed to raise consciousness (female and male) and promote the cause of human equity in art, culture and life in general. Anne wanted us to meet her family, and her colleagues at KNOW, place a few books in some Pittsburgh stores, and perhaps do a TV interview. This was all too much to resist.

Out of Buffalo we rolled down I-90 to Erie, then south on I-79 toward Pittsburgh. Despite the next immediate experience, Pennsylvania remains one eastern state which gives me wonder, an unruly sentience of monumental hardwood expanses, great rain mountains and full-running rivers. Pennsylvania reminds me of the best from the Nineteenth Century, and when I hear old river songs I think of it. The cities, like all other cities, are smoke traps, but for now Pennsylvania is rugged good old land.

It was a moonless night and we possessed no decent map of Pittsburgh. We entered from the north, worked our way to the city center to get its feel, then worked northeast along the south bank of the Allegheny. Our main target was Wilkinsburg, which we could see on our little map far to the south and straight east of the city. But nothing resembling a southward route presented itself, and before we knew it we were hopelessly befuddled along the dark roads, angular enough to make any Vermonter gleeful, around an Allegheny River town called Oakmont. Nor could we find a map either—which reminds me to say that coast to coast and heaven to hell from the smallest independent gas pump to the grandest big-company station the oilmen are failures when it comes to maps—or anything else, really, except maybe gasoline. If you have the need, the time and the guts for it, don't buy from a station that can't deliver a map, or a restroom, or a window wash. It's a cynical business anyway, oil, and during 1974 it was worse than usual because it was a seller's market. If you fill up and *then* discover the joint has no maps, you're stuck with prying one loose from a place from which you can make no purchase, and the story often is that "we reserve the maps for our customers." We took the offensive on this, however, and usually asked how much they'd sell a map for (it's called Middle-Class Guilt Avoidance). Even this didn't always work, though once Ellen got a horselaugh (and a free map) out of a guy who seemed to sense her angst.

Angst was all around Oakmont that night. We found one station open in ten miles of Allegheny River road, and that a rotting Sunoco with a three-bit punk attendant who, when I asked for a map looked at me as though I'd asked for a malted milk. Shortly after that something chewed loose in a rear wheel, and a voice from under our seats nagged "What'd you expect after this many miles?" We parked on a hill while I felt the hubs for heat. No heat. Brakes? We still had some. "We may never get loose of these hills," I whimpered as we clanked away, and for awhile it looked just that way. For two hours we tried to find our way onto I-76 which we could see on the infernally infinitesimal map slicing south into the city of Monroeville. We passed under that interstate what seemed like forty times but access was apparently limited to zero. Finally we stopped near the town of Unity and I went into a local bar. I slid onto a stool between what looked to be natives. The guy on my right explained in meticulous detail, drawing a map with his finger; the guy on my left said nothing until it was over, then he nudged me and mumbled "That aint right, what he says."

I dismounted from the stool as an argument ensued. "Is it *close?*"

"Yeh—but it aint *right.*"

"Close will do me," I said.

But it didn't. Thirty minutes later we pulled into a laundromat, and this time Ellen did it. The old man doing his wash at 2 AM was also meticulous, and we finally got into the town of Monroeville without ever locating the interstate. Our trek through the close-stacked Pennsylvania hills was punctuated with periodic grindings in the rear wheel, closing up our priorities for the next day. At a motel that night we were too road-weary to copy names out of the yellow pages. We ripped out the pages and felt so criminally good that we also ripped out a city map to boot.

The map got us into the center of Pittsburgh with some cognition about the lay of the town. It is tucked into the notch where the Ohio, the Allegheny and the Monongahela converge (hence such small press names as Three Rivers Press), and the main traffic arteries from east to west all vector into that ever-tightening notch until you are downtown. The streets narrow as you go, and the buildings grow higher, while a seeming south-to-north tilt to the place would make for vertigo—if you had time in the traffic. To appreciate the quaint charm of this city you need to be afoot, for the single-lane traffic on every street demands full concentration, and is perilous even then.

Anne Pride had lined up two TV interviews for the next day, one for early morning, another at 1 PM, both on network television. The PM show was called the Marie Torre Show during which a fine person named Marie Torre interviewed authors about books. We used this information in downtown Pittsburgh that first day and managed to get books into two stores, one a huge department store, Kauffman's, whose proprietor knew novels and was interested in small presses. We left the big stores at mid-city feeling we probably should have done better, thinking we might have leaned too single-dimensionedly on the morrow's TV showings. Booksellers have been around. They know it takes more than an hour's worth of TV to peddle an unknown book. They know how evanescent an author's promotion can be. They needed to hear more about the lasting saleability of the thing, and in concentrating on the TV shows we probably failed to give them that.

The shows went well, however. In the AM Anne, myself and a small newspaper publisher were interviewed about small presses, agents, distribution and so forth. In the afternoon the Marie Torre Show was themed on "The West", and four of us with books out on the subject were eventually crowded onto a small stage—along with Marie. It seemed curious to be doing that in an eastern industrial town half a continent away from Bozeman or Ten Sleep; but on the other hand it was there and yet farther east where lay the fiscal might and main now making high plains controversy. It was good if often haphazard dialogue, and as the only one contributing a work of fiction I was able for once to play the role of artist—except for an admonishment about small press publishing at the end, to which one of the others responded "You won't get *me* to defend big publishers!"

Later that afternoon we visited the University of Pittsburgh Bookstore which knew our work and much else going on in small press publishing, knew about the New York Book Fair, COSMEP, the *Whole COSMEP Catalog*, and the Directory. Shortly we took the largest order of the entire trip, over $80 worth of books.

We toured Pittsburgh, which has some fine old sections, spent an hour or two at the KNOW office talking with Joann Gardner and the others about publishing problems and things in general. KNOW is larger than most small presses, with six or seven employees, but it runs in the same personal, homey way. We spent a delightful evening with Anne and her family, and her husband Ed, a silk-screen printer, is a knockout cook, talker, golfer, and person. Anne and I talked for an hour or more into a tape recorder about publishing—only to find that the recorder was defective. She now possessed an excuse to come to California!

We were loathe to leave Pittsburgh because of the friends we'd met there in two days, and because we rather liked that big, busy city as against the fifty others we'd seen in a month. It had character still, despite its half-million population and its great industrial commerce. And it lived amid some of the finest looking country in the east.

XI. Cornbasket

We drove toward a midwestern drought, and we knew it. Central Ohio was born hot, but in July it can raise blisters on your feet and on your mind and there's no telling where it hurts most. In Columbus cool water was as scarce as football fans were thick and the only oases were icecream shacks. We found the last Friendly's Ice Cream Parlor going west, and had to call upon the bottommost reserves of motivation to re-enter the sun blizzard.

There are some fifteen bookstores here (and 530,000 people) and I suspect in the right season you could sell some books. But a summer Saturday is not that season. The main street past the University is High Street, and we started from its city-center source and worked our way back for five miles until the stores ran out. Many operators were not in, but the feeling clung to us like the hot carseat that that was not our true dilemma. One block west on Neil we U-turned to visit yet another Little Professor Book Center, hoping it might change our luck as it had several times before. But some things you don't do, like spit into the wind—or fool Columbus with a fancy turn. A scud of portending smoke floated out from under the carhood, an inspection revealed that the power steering cable was punctured, and under pressure (such as in a turn) spewed fluid forth directly onto the fire-hot exhaust manifold. Hence, smoke. And, just as the birth of power is the death of sex, so when machine troubles start does bookselling expire.

A retrospective anecdote: A small press friend, Dan Dorman, editor of Cider Press, lives in Columbus. We might have visited with him, but now did not wish to come bearing problems. When Dorman later read of our troubles in Columbus he called and said, "Do you know what I do to support my publishing? I sell auto parts!"

That's the way Ohio was.

But the University there is big enough to be almost anything to anyone. The library has an immense small mag/press collection, which I think we would have gained more by visiting than by bookselling on the streets.

That evening it rained as we circled Indianapolis. The real drought was just west of the Illinois line, as we learned when we arrived in Champaign. Even in Indianapolis the rain was as thick as spittle, rather gum-like in the air than lubricating, rather some great rainmaker's cyclic contempt than nutrient gift. One of these times, because we pressure the earth so, this cycle of contempt will kill us.

In Champaign our friend, Bob Schneider, a prof at Illinois and an intense gardener, acknowledged that the drought upon the belly of the American cornbasket was truly onerous. You could irrigate, though the quality diminished without new rain, but there was nothing like skywater for growing.

We sold books at Follett's and at The Used Bookstore, and on a hunch I visited the Champaign-Urbana News Gazette. There I found a young Montana man, Rodger Cramer, who grinned and said sure he'd write a thing. I'd heard that, too, but the fact is that Cramer did come through, and in style, with one of the better reviews of *The Grassman*.

We visited Ruthie Wantling in Normal up the line, and talked of her poet-man Bill who'd died the previous May, and who'd been a friend/brother to me for over ten years. Ruthie was getting along, making a space for herself, planning some travel. I had published Bill Wantling's *The Source* in '66. He was a true person, a musician of the soul who'd ridden some hard horses all his 41 years and yet kept returning to the music, to the soul. Since *The Source* his books had been published in England and New Zealand, though his final short work, *7 On Style*, was published by Second Coming this year.

Quietly then we moved out of Illinois into Iowa, leaving the flat, dry cornland and encountering the rolling, dry cornland. I remembered my first trek through here in the fifties, driving a wreck of a Willys across the very bottom of the state, starting in

Fort Madison and winding up in Nebraska City, catching every white-sand road and detour in between, non-stop from New York to Lincoln.

Iowa City we thought should be good, but the place was either closed for the summer or under construction. I sold some Directories at the Iowa Book and Supply, but the University Bookstore was sealed up for inventory, and the fellow at Epstein's waved me out without hearing a word.

"It's back in the midwest," said Ellen when we started feeling fitful again.

Des Moines was worse, 200,000 people, six stores (for a .03 stores-per-thousand mark) and a cross-hatch street grid. I sold one book, and that to a woman running a used bookstore who had no business buying it. Downtown, which cost nerve getting to, there was no way they would speculate on an unknown book; and across from Drake University I locked claws with another proprietor who would not complicate life with further knowledge (BIP, I restfully concede this measure of ground—for now.)

And that was Iowa.

We drew into Omaha that night, conscious that we were still east of the magic ninety-eighth meridian, but hoping to fool the devil all the same. Here is where the drought was pulverizing the land. The corn was three feet up and fully tasseled, and already they were plowing it under in places. "We got two weeks, and that's it for the whole crop," one man told me. "If it rains before then it might fill out and come on up." The country was into a truly diabolical phase; the drought followed excessive rain in May and June, which raised hell with the season's start. A double whammy.

We cased the city, getting its lay for the next morning, then drove west out of town and found a low-priced motel. In the morning the sky had wrinkled up and a mean wind cut in from the northwest. *Maybe it can do it*, I thought, eyeing the runted cornfields. It started and stopped for three or four hours, but never got far and finally burned off.

None of the Omaha city-center stores would listen to bookselling in that weather. Nearer the river an old industrial area was being reclaimed by young craft-merchants lodging themselves and their wares into old boxcars, freight stations and railroad offices, and here I finally sold a couple of books. Back out on Dodge at the University of Nebraska-Omaha Bookstore I fell into conversation with Ben Koenig, the manager, about some open·land he'd just bought around Council Bluffs. I inferred that Iowa land was cheaper than Nebraska, and when I'd argued price with a motelman the evening before he'd told me to "go across the river" if I wanted something cheap—"they'll sell anything over there." The river, the Missouri, apparently divides this area socio-economically.

We decided to leave a review copy with Victor Haas at the Omaha World Herald, and traipsed back down Dodge into the middle of town. As I pulled up across from the newspaper building to back into the one parking place in sight a woman snugged up behind me and refused to back off. I was unable to tuck the car into place. I thought maybe she herself was jammed up, but there wasn't another car moving on the street. Ellen got out and walked back as the woman closed and locked everything in sight, then opened a window an inch for long enough to shout "You can't back up in this city!"
The drought was more than weather.
Moments later, when I confronted an armed barricade in the lobby of the World Herald I asked if it was indeed illegal to back up in Omaha. Almost as soon as I'd said it, of course, the ludicrousness of it struck, and the armed barricade and I had a fair laugh. I did not, needless to say, get in to see Haas.

By the time we reached Lincoln the sun was back to its full mean power again, and I knew the North Platte, a river which lay above ground water, would be nothing but white Nebraska sand. Lincoln itself proved unyielding in more ways than the sun, and after rassling with day-end traffic and several kinds of cul-de-sacs we threaded our way out of town, stopping at Nebraska Wesleyan University to use the bathroom.

I was reminded on this long, straight, white road of a rather seminal trip I'd managed to the Ann Arbor COSMEP Conference in '69 with Jerry Burns (Goliards) and Richard Morris, the org's coordinator. We had an old station wagon with a bed laid out in the rear. Richard didn't drive—still doesn't—so Jerry and I alternated behind the wheel and sacked out astern, denying Richard the bed most of the time. About here, in mid-Nebraska going east, a sudden flu struck me as I was trying to get a wink or two, and finally I called Burns to stop, the Laramie dinner we'd eaten a while ago was about to land on Nebraska—or down his neck if he kept driving.

I got out, heaved, and then walked half a mile or so listening to the tall corn along either side.

"Sorry," I said when I got back in the car.

"Hell," said Burns, "Nebraska will turn it all back into groceries by morning!"

I thought about that now as I watched the shrunken corn go by. It'd probably take whatever it could get at this point.

Two hours out of Lincoln the northwestern Nebraska sky mounted the damndest stack of vermillion-black clouds I'd seen since a Salt Flats blow five years earlier. They churned and unravelled up off the plains like a menacing cape, and the horizon disappeared in a kind of misty turmoil. The cattle all along faced away from it, southeast, waiting, and in moments the entire visual world closed down around us in solid curtains of skywater, bringing the universe to a dead stop. It was a merry thing, though it was much too hard, and it vanished as swiftly as it had come.

Two hours after that I asked a man out near Ogallala if he'd seen some weather.

"I aint seen rain for two months," he knifed.

The North Platte was white.

XII. The Eye of the Sun

In *The Grassman* Cheyenne figures. It bears a kind of threatening, evil lever on the novel's water conflict, generates slick cattle politicians backed by henskin-slickered Texans, and becomes synonymous with corporate-imperial power mongering. There was a day when a self-appointed band of barons called the Stock Growers Association ruled the territory with iron and lead, and in that day Cheyenne earned every notch of its bloody political name.

Now it is only slightly political, somewhat military, and full of gas stations and eat-fast restaurants. Its rodeo each year ranks with Calgary and Pendleton as one of the three best. It sits in a kind of saucer of earth, and the sun and wind bang into it, rattling its shutters and signs until you swear primordial spirits walk its skies.

We pulled into a phone booth on the city's eastern edge and Ellen went in to check out some stores. Just yonder was a gas station, and as I watched I saw two youths making it out of there in a stealthy half-crouch for their bikes, which were parked not ten feet from my car. When they were near the bikes I noticed what they'd stolen. I leaned out the window.

"Hey fellas," I said in my best growl, "is that a map?"

They might have been ten, and they froze, turned sheepishly and nodded.

Wyoming?"

They brightened some, half nodded. I looked beside me on the seat.

"Trade you for Nebraska?"

More than one way to skin the petrogods!

We sold books at two of Cheyenne's three stores, and I visited with Red Kelso on the Wyoming Eagle.

"It won't really be a review," he said frankly, passing the book back to me and keeping the dustjacket. "I'll probably just steal a little info from the flap."

I understood—but gave him back the book.

"Who knows, you might get into it one of these winter nights!"

It was fifty miles over the hump into Laramie, where I'd spent some of my best years. The hump was 8,000 feet, and I could recall some fairly deadly winter passages over it. It was high, dry country all around, sheep country, lightly timbered with pine clumps and shot with dry draws. You could drop down into Laramie (elevation 7,200) across a barren plain. The Snowy Range stands in the west exuding a certain majesty and promise that must have drawn the early pioneers on like a lodestar. Stored cold water.

Laramie is an oasis in the endless red-brown grasslands. Not only does it have water but trees—which are fast disappearing. As an alumnus I received a brochure in 1970 citing "ten years of progress" at the University. What they meant by that was *construction*, and the brochure cover was an aerial shot of the campus in 1960, and another in 1970. It proved that progress and trees do not mix. I was going to publish it with an article by Peter Michelson, about his experience in coming here in 1969 to publish a small magazine for the University (he lasted less than a year) but Michelson never got the article together.

Laramie had been a marker for me back there in the late fifties. Hell, I know the fragility of a psychogeography—"you can take the boy out of the farm but you can't take the farm out of the boy" (I first heard that from a city slicker who didn't know a farm from a frigate)—and yet that remains for me the natural nut of literature, certainly of *The Grassman*, and of my own life. A sense of *place* and my own relation to it, however short the tenancy there, is the thing that makes the novel a workable genre, a "sluggish" genre, as Jose Ortega Y Gassett has called it. I think I understood this about life itself when I arrived in Laramie, though perhaps not at that point did I understand it about the novel.

On this July day in 1974 the University had already stocked copies of *The Grassman*. I sold them Directories, we visited a friend, left books at a store called "Books A-Go-Go" whose owner insisted that the last book about Wyoming to come in had sold over

500 copies. I felt somewhat wry, and probably looked it, suggested that we make somewhat more modest assumptions about this novel. Later I left a gift copy with the Albany County librarian, who gave it a brief review in the local paper. And then as the ground haze rose to meet the coming night we drove into the eye of the mythic red sun.

Like Nebraska, Wyoming used to take a day to cross—and once weeks. Now of course you can burn the place down and leave a smogtrail from Bosler to the Green River in under four hours if you're crazy. But now you had to work in the 55-MPH factor, which stretched out any trip, and which coincidentally make the interstates safer and saner. I believe in fact that this was the first cross-country trip (of many) in which I did not witness the afterwreckage of some horrendous auto accident. Every place had its psychosexual weakling with a lead foot, but generally it seemed that people traveled at more gentle speeds. Of the states I would mark for good driving: Oregon, South Dakota, Maine; those for bad: Connecticut, Illinois, Nevada. The cities, east, west or midwest, where any given pathology runs its virulent best, is where you encounter the worst.

After an evening traversing the prehistoric southern red plains of Wyoming, and a night in the dusty cornertown of Evanston (hideaway home of Wyoming's only State Hospital), we made Salt Lake City at the crest of a new and burning sun. It was over one hundred degrees, and the bitter-hot desert air slung low agains the city's border-to-border pavement. It was a spiritual ordeal by furnace, a test of the will as a great, gold Moroni watched from the center of town—and a test, too, not incidentally of the faculty to understand street numbers. For Salt Lake is laid out in a grid extending north, south, east and west from Moroni, with the north-south numbers labeled "east" and "west", and the east-west numbers labeled "north" and "south". It is the most logical and defiant system we encountered on the entire trip, and we spent some time fathoming it. As we plodded, dry, from one block a thousand feet to the next I would often hallucinate a high and distant bleat, as of a trumpet, and glance back up the hill toward the yellow angel. Of the fifteen or so stores in this town there are probably five good ones; we sold books at both the University Bookstore (see Lester Perry) and the Utah College

Bookstore, and got promises (as yet unfulfilled) from the Deseret Bookstore and Zion, the latter with the best western collection I think we'd encountered.

Later we thought to take a swim in the great Salt Lake (everyone should do it once) but the crowds and sand fleas dissuaded us. On the white Flats later we hiked out onto the salt crust with a storm mounting in the northern sky, then drove out toward Bonneville until the road died away, as our long bookselling trip was about to do in the sparsening western drycountry. And as we crossed Nevada through Wells, Elko and Winnemucca other names, places and people were beginning to have a settled meaning in our memories, and this particular travelogue took rudimentary shape. We'd seen ten thousand miles of American Road and we didn't want to lose it with the last mile. As the Sierra bumped up in front of us we knew, as surely as we knew we'd be glad for home, that we would be re-running that ten thousand miles in all its sound and color for many cold moons to come.

Appendix A: Trip Summary

In this tabulation the states are arranged alphabetically with each city visited given within state. City populations are given, number of stores (according to our information), plus the number of stores per thousand of population (no. of stores divided by one thousandth of population shown). Also shown: number of stores in each city which took books from us, number of books sold in that particular city, and the dollar value of books according to our invoices. In the next-to-last column each city has been rated (A through F), and an average sale computed ($ divided by number of stores buying).

As to the ratings, these have been assigned impressionistically on the basis of sales, notes and memories concerning traffic conditions, treatment, food, and general sense of the worth of our time and energy in having gone into the city. On another trip, e.g., we would definitely visit the A's and B's again, avoid the D's and F's, and visit the C's if time and circumstance permitted.

See also notes at end of table.

State/City	Population	No. of Stores	Stores Per M
California			
Red Bluff	7600	1	.13
Redding	16600	1	.06
Tahoe City	1400	1	.71
Yreka	5400	1	.19
Connecticut			
Storrs	10700	1	.09
Willimantic	14400	1	.07
Idaho			
Coeur d'Alene	16200	3	.19
Illinois			
Champaign/ Urbana	56500	11	.19
Indiana			
South Bend	125600	10	.08
Iowa			
Iowa City	46800	5	.11
Des Moines	200600	6	.03
Maine			
York Beach	900	1	1.11
Ogunquit	800	1	1.25
Kennebunkport	1100	1	.91
Portland	65100	6	.09
Falmouth	6300	3	.48
Massachusetts			
Springfield	163900	5	.03
Westfield	31400	1	.03
Minnesota			
Albert Lea/ Austin, etc.	44500	4	.09
Montana			
Big Timber	1600	1	.63
Billings	61600	3	.05
Bozeman	18700	4	.21
Butte	23400	1	.04
Deer Lodge	15600	1	.06
Livingston	6900	1	.14
Missoula	29500	7	.24

No. of Stores Buying	No. of Books Sold	$	Rating	$ Per Sale
1	4	9.48	B	9.48
1	1	1.77	C	1.77
1	10	23.70	B	23.70
1	3	5.31	C	5.31
1	6	8.91	C	8.91
1	11	28.47	A	28.47
2	10	18.90	B	9.45
2	7	17.19	C	8.60
1	5	8.10	D	8.10
1	5	14.85	D	14.85
1	1	1.77	D	1.77
1	3	5.31	B	5.31
1	2	3.54	B	3.54
0	0	0	D	0
0	0	0	E	0
1	5	8.95	A	8.95
3	11	19.47	C	6.49
1	5	10.05	B	10.05
0	0	0	D	0
1	2	3.54	B	3.54
2	13	25.44	C	12.72
3	32	73.26	A	24.42
1	6	10.62	C	10.62
0	0	0	B	0
0	0	0	C	0
2	7	12.39	C	6.20

Nebraska			
Lincoln	149500	6	.04
Omaha	347300	9	.03
Nevada			
Reno	72900	6	.08
New Hampshire			
Keene	20500	2	.10
Manchester/ Bedford	87800	8	.09
New York			
Buffalo	462800	17	.04
Middletown	22600	2	.09
Syracuse	197200	8	.04
Ohio			
Columbus	539700	15	.03
Oregon			
Albany	18200	3	.16
Ashland	12300	5	.41
Corvalis	35100	4	.11
Eugene	76300	13	.17
Medford	28400	5	.18
Newport	5200	1	.19
Portland	382600	28	.07
Salem	68300	4	.06
The Dalles	10400	2	.19
Pennsylvania			
Pittsburgh	520100	16	.03
South Dakota			
Deadwood	2400	1	.42
Lead	5400	1	.19
Rapid City	43800	4	.09
Sioux Falls	72500	7	.10
Spearfish	4700	2	.43
Wall	800	1	1.25
Utah			
Salt Lake City	175900	16	.09
Vermont			
Brattleboro	12200	2	.16
Burlington	38600	7	.18
Montpelier	8600	1	.12

0	0	0	E	0
2	13	34.44	C	17.22
1	6	11.82	C	11.82
1	3	5.31	C	5.31
3	11	19.47	B	6.49
3	41	82.17	A	27.39
1	5	11.25	B	11.25
1	5	8.85	D	8.85
0	0	0	E	0
2	9	17.13	B	8.57
0	0	0	D	0
3	29	66.93	A	22.31
6	42	102.60	A	17.10
0	0	0	D	0
1	5	11.25	B	11.25
3	17	37.66	B	12.55
1	6	8.91	D	8.91
1	2	5.30	C	5.30
3	89	127.05	B	42.35
0	0	0	C	0
1	2	6.54	B	6.54
2	16	60.77	B	30.39
3	61	104.49	B	34.83
2	11	21.87	B	10.94
0	0	0	C	0
2	10	27.30	C	13.65
1	2	3.54	C	3.54
3	20	44.43	B	14.81
1	5	11.25	A	11.25

Washington			
Kenniwick/ Pasco/ Richland	55400	2	.04
Spokane	170500	12	.07
Wisconsin			
LaCrosse	51200	7	.14
Madison	173300	16	.09
Wyoming			
Buffalo	3400	1	.29
Big Horn	500	1	2.00
Casper	39400	4	.10
Cheyenne	40900	3	.07
Laramie	23100	3	.13
Sheridan	10800	1	.09
TOTALS—	4,963,700	329	.07

Inferencing ⟶

0	0	0	D	0
1	5	11.25	C	11.25
2	10	23.80	C	11.90
2	10	27.66	D	13.83
1	10	29.70	B	29.70
0	0	0	B	0
3	15	32.55	B	10.85
2	9	21.93	B	10.97
2	16	44.84	B	22.42
0	0	0	C	0
91	636	1333.08	—	14.65

2.48% of U.S. population (of 200,000,000).
This puts 13,000 to 14,000 bookstores in the country, say 13,500.
27.6% bought books (91/329)
So of the 13,500, 3726 would buy books.
We sold an average of 7 books per sale (636/91)
Hence, 3726 sales X 7 = 26,082 books.
Our average sale was $14.65, and average per-book sale was $2.10.
Hence, 3726 sales X 14.65 = 54,585.00; and
    26082 books X 2.10 = 54,772.00.
We covered 6.5 stores per day (275 stores in 42 days), and made 2.2 sales per day.
Hence, it would take 1693 days to cover U.S. (5 years for 1 person, 1 year for 5, etc.)
We sold about one-third of the stores we visited: (2.2/6.5, or 91/275).

etc

Appendix B: Annotated List of Bookstores

RED BLUFF, CA 96080

MIDDLE EARTH BOOKS, 643 Main St. Mother/daugther management; receptive to new, small presses. Neither a large store nor a large city (7,600). There is in this store an air of interest in the world of books, and in general. Took Grassman and Directory and expressed interest in COSMEP Catalog.

REDDING, CA 96001

HYATT'S BOOKSTORE, 230 Hilltop Drive. Small to medium in size; proprietor (Mrs. Hyatt) very sensitive and knowledgeable. Much "whole earth" material, some hardbacks. She asked to read the Grassman before ordering, has since paid for it but not ordered more....

YREKA, CA 96097

TRANS BOOK CO., 223 West Miner St. This is part of a chain with main offices at 590 Folsom St., San Francisco, 94105. I don't know how many stores are involved, but there is individual ordering and central billing. Proprietor, young and bright, claimed "nothing was selling" and "everyone wanted paperbacks." Took 3 Grassmans and an interest in COSMEP Catalog. I suggest sending promo material to central offices.

ASHLAND, OR 97520

GOLDEN MEAN BOOKSTORE, 1253 Siskiyou. Small, mostly religious and occult, some American Indian (though not a lot). Receptive to local authors (Jackson and Douglas Counties?) but otherwise not adventuresome.

THE MART, 270 East Main St. Combination stationary; all Modern Library Editions.

McCARLEY'S BOOKS, 161 East Main St. Slick, small-to-medium sized, much traffic and some good how-to titles. According to McCarley, however, "the tourists didn't come this year," indicating his trade is mainly out-of-towners to the famous Shakespeare Festival. But I might've been getting the heave-ho.

SOUTHERN OREGON BOOK CO., 88 North Main St. Small, looked generally prospective but managers were out, in fact, were "rarely in." I half suspect a tourist den of it.

SOUTHERN OREGON COLLEGE BOOKSTORE, c/o S.O.C. Manager takes long lunch.

MEDFORD, OR 97501

BARTLETTS, 1616 South Bartlett. Almost all used, though sometimes carries new books, some mags. I looked for a book which someday I'll find, Clay Fisher's **Red Blizzard**, and in the process came to feel that the books were stacked and handled carelessly. So made no firm pitch.

BOOKLANDS, 130 East Main St. Jerry Baird, prop. Moving to new location and suggested he would order something then. Probably the best prospect in town.

BOOKS PRIMARILY, 528 East Main St. Bob and Jean Zaddock. Used books only but just starting. Who knows? Friendly port in an auto-storm.

J.K. Gill Co., Shopping Center. This is a chain of somewhat middle-classy bookstores rigged for quick sale, mostly. Often has good selection of Western Americana. Must be approached through Michael Brasky, 2725 N.W. Industrial, Portland, OR. In August I visited Brasky, again sensed a volume-consciousness, and left him some books. Several orders for the COSMEP Catalog have been forthcoming, inspired, I suspect, by individual customers, not my visit. I think the samples I left have fallen into idleness.

SWEMS, 217 East Main St. Almost all hardback, non-fiction, with **Mother Earth News** front and center. Small part of a small department store. Good selection on the west, Indians, local subjects and authors.

EUGENE, OR 97403

BOOK AND TEA SHOP, 1846 East 19th Ave. Lodged in a revamped private home, yet jammed with good titles for a very small shop. Good women's section, some expensive stuff. Has stocked COSMEP Catalog. Took 5 Grassman on consignment, plus 2 Directories.

BOOK FAIR, 1409 Oak St. Used, mostly; otherwise somewhat tendentious about "what sells" and what doesn't.

BOOK MART, 856 Olive St. Mrs Crafts, Prop. Medium in size in downtown shopping mall. From appearance, gives full space to major publishers.

THE BOOK PEOPLE, 2455 Hilyard St. Susan and Dick Klynn, Props. Small shop in tiny shopping center; some good knowledge of books in general. Took 2 of the novel, 2 Directories. I think they'd stock s-p titles limitedly.

CLIMAX BOOK SHOP, 60 West 13th St. Porn—you can usually tell by the name. Almost every city has some, and these are not really **book** people, but tough, often jaded, often impatient, fast-buck artists. I pitched this one (as I did several along the way) and got a grin out of the woman proprietor—the kind of grin you'd expect if you tried to trade in a horse on a used car.

HOUSE OF CRAFTS, 642 Polk St. Advertises books but carries very few. A home operation, mostly needlework, if I remember. Craft books, like those of Running Press, might go here.

THE ID, Alder & 13th St. Near university, hip and crowded. Should be a natural for small press titles, but I dunno. I visited twice but couldn't entice the manager out of his back office to say hello either time.

THE KIVA, 136 East 11th St. Exists in resurrected warehouse or factory with other craft merchants, health food, etc. Nice selection of books. Friendly and interested, but manager was out.

THE LITERARY LION, 84 East Broadway. In downtown shopping mall, with second location at 2835 Oak St. Medium sized, many hardbacks and some expensive titles. Somewhat open attitude. Took 5 Grassmans and mused at Directory and COSMEP Catalog. Paid.

UNIVERSITY OF OREGON BOOKSTORE, P.O. Box 3176. Man to see is young J. West. Novels are tough to sell in college bookstores as two-year buffalo chips. Here, he took the directory, and I liked it. But always try these stores—I made some astounding sales places like Bozeman, Sioux Falls, Pittsburgh, Burlington, Omaha. You can also get into some good raps.

THE SMITH FAMILY BOOKSTORE, 1233 Alder. This is where the dry spell (from Ashland and Medford) ended—over $30 worth of books, including hardbacks and Directories. New venture, just shaping up an old place, retired garbageman now in books. Many used, just getting into new. Wide taste, good place for small presses to beat Random House (store not listed in yellow pages.)

SON OF KOOBDOOGA BOOKS, 651 East 13th St. In my experience via mail this **is** the small-press shop in Eugene. Carries whole spectrum of titles, has excellent women's section, how-to, good range of poetry. Was selling Nixon Transcripts at cost. Stocks Whole COSMEP Catalog and all Dustbooks Directories.

WALDEN BOOKSTORES, 234 River Valley Center. They give you the notion, these outfits, that all ordering is centrally initiated, but the fact is that a number of Walden stores (and Dalton and Gill too) have ordered COSMEP Catalog, apparently at a customer's request. Don't fight it. Go to Stamford, Connecticut and see the big man. Paul Foreman did with Grassman and took a good order.

CORVALLIS, OR 97330

CORL'S, 495 S.W. Madison. Most prospective, straight, general-audience store in Corvallis. Took 4 Grassmans, 2 Directories. Small to medium in size, some hardbacks, magazines. Prop. (Mr. Corl) is down-to-earth fellow.

GOLDEN TORTOISE, 110 N.W. Van Buren. All used, some mags. Spare, uninspiring.

GRASS ROOTS, 227 S.W. 2nd. Small and hip; good how-to, women, ecology, some poetry but manager claims it's "hard to sell" and won't stock much. Took 2 of the novel, one **Directory.**

OREGON STATE UNIVERSITY BOOKSTORE, Memorial Union, O.S.U. See Mrs. Finnegan. Hard to find in huge campus but Mrs. F. very receptive to new titles. Promised to send order after new fiscal year—and **did**. Large store, wide variety. **Never** assume (as I once did) that these stores handle only textbooks, or are interested in students alone. The larger they are the more they tend to conceive of themselves as part of the business community.

VARSITY BOOK EXCHANGE, N.W. 26th and N.W. Monroe. Closing and moving.

ALBANY, OR 97321

BOOK EXCHANGE, 138 West First. A basement shop, closed until PM. Possibly Porn.

DUEDALL-POTTS STATIONERY STORE, 343 West First (P.O. Box 9). Ellen handled this one; three Christian women went through copies of Grassman page by page for printing flaws. Took three, finally, and paid for them. More stationery than books.

PLEIADES, 110 South Ferry. This was a pleasant find, a proprietor very interested in small-press publishing. Much non-commercial material; non-slick layout. Excellent prospect for small presses in general.

SALEM, OR 97301

THE BOOK RACK, 1107 Edgewater N.W. Very tiny, almost all used.

CAMBRIDGE BOOKSTORE, Lancaster Mall.
"Your name isn't Michener, is it?"
"No—thank gawd!"
"Sorry."

PAPERBACK EXCHANGE, 357 State St. All used—up: books, people, air.

WILLAMETTE UNIVERSITY BOOKSTORE. Ray Naas, Mgr. Nice store, many non-text titles. Won't buy unknown novels. Took Directories.

NOTE ON SALEM: For its size (68,300) this

city is a disaster for both traffic and bookstores. There are, in addition to the above stores, three Christian (Bible) shops and two porn joints, plus other second hand stores. Also there's a place called The Gallery Book Store at 609 Court, Dallas, OR 97338; a Pat's Bookery at 500 South Capitol Way, Olympia (wherever that is); and a McCleag Country Store at 8342 McCleag Rd. S.E. (Salem?). We visited none of these.

PORTLAND, OR 97200

NOTE: We slipped past Portland on the first run, but in late August returned to attend and take part in the Second Annual Portland Poetry Festival, and spent a day on the street at that time. In late '74 Dustbooks published a novel (**The Honey Dwarf**) by Portland writer Gene Detro and many more stores opened up to us. The following comments include in some cases that later experience.

THE ALTERNATIVE, 221 S.W. Pine.

APACHE BOOKS & BEDKNOBS, 631 S.E. Morrison.

ARMCHAIR FAMILY BOOKSTORE, 3205 S.E. Milwaukee.

FRED N. BAY NEWS CO., 3155 N.W. Yeon Ave., Wholesaler.

BIRDS AND BEES, 12346 S.E. Division.

BLACK EDUCATIONAL CENTER BOOKSTORE, 3703 N. Williams.

THE BOOK CELLAR, 267 "A" Avenue, Lake Oswego. James Swingford, Mgr. Good selection and good bet for small presses.

BOOK HAVEN, 4940 N. Lombard.

BOOK & RECORD SHOP, 3638 S.E. Hawthorne Blvd.

THE BOOK VAULT, 3125 S.W. Cedar Hills Blvd., Beaverton. Jane Melhvish, Mgr. Small store, but awake.

THE BOOKWORM, 4120 N.E. Sandy Blvd.

BRIAN THOMAS BOOKS, 822 S.W. 10th. Carries many Dustbooks titles. A top-notch small press store in the heart of Portland.

B. DALTON, 530 S.W. 5th (downtown).

B. DALTON, 1004 Lloyd Center. Carl Grath, Mgr.

B. DALTON, 9720 S.W. Washington Square Road. Susan Grath, Mgr.

Note on Dalton: The only business we do with Dalton here is with Detro's **Honey Dwarf,** and that because of that author's insistence, ingenuity and importance in Portland bookselling. I repeat myself of earlier in these annotations: **if** you have a local author you're probably in—otherwise it's off to Minneapolis (& I have yet to see even that pay off).

J.K. GILL CO., 408 S.W. 5th Street. This is one of a chain of many small stores in the northwest, usually in shopping malls. Books are only part of the ware, and in my experience the whole operation is overrated as far as bookselling is concerned. Samples should be sent to Michael Brasky, 2725 N.W. Industrial (phone 226-4611), but don't expect either speed **or** the books back.

GREAT BOOKS OF THE WESTERN WORLD, 1235 N.E. 10th.

THE GREEN DOLPHIN, 215 S.W. Ankeny.

LOOKING GLASS BOOKSTORE, 421 S.W.

Taylor. Many small press titles—a good bet all around.

MARY'S BOOKS, 401 W. Burnside.

PORTLAND STATE UNIVERSITY BOOKSTORE, 531 S.W. Hall. A nice buch of folks. Sensitive to small press works, women, third world, etc. One of the early stores to stock COSMEP Catalog.

PORTLAND COMMUNITY COLLEGE BOOKSTORE, 1200 S.W. 49th Avenue. Carries Directory regularly.

WALT POWELL BOOKS, 302 S.W. 12th. Very small but right-on.

REP BOOK CENTER, 1405 S.W. 17th.

SOMETHING OWL BOOKSTORE, 7828 S.W. 35th Phil Huber, Mgr. New store, coming on.

VARSITY BOOK EXCHANGE, 1909 S.W. 6th. Across from Portland State U. Promised to order COSMEP Catalog but never did.

VOLUME 1, 100018 S.E. Washington.

WOMAN'S PLACE, 706 S.E. Grand.

NEWPORT, OR 97365

CANYON WAY BOOKSTORE, 1216 S.W. Canyon Way. Slightly on tourist side, but a nice place. Stocked COSMEP Catalog and **Grassman.**

THE DALLES, OR 97058

CRAIG OFFICE SUPPLY, 308 Washington St. The buyer is Beverly Craig, who claimed last summer to be overstocked. At best, mostly Oregon/Washington (local) material will go here, though is generally interested in books of all sorts. Many such office suppliers are spiritually booksellers—but make a living in pencils, wrapping paper, note pads. That eventually may have a die-back effect on their bookselling, though it can go the other way too.

WEIGELT BROS. BOOKSTORE, 414 Federal St. Dim-lit, homey. Local material has a good chance here. If you're ready to horsetrade in small quantities the proprietor will take consignment and 10%.

PASCO, WA 99301

BOOKLAND, 329 West Lewis. Fair sized newsstand with many periodicals. Straight commerce.

SHIELDS BOOK & STATIONERY, 420 West Lewis. See Mrs. Shields at this address, but main outlet seems to be at 533 Columbia Center Mall, Kennewick 99336.

SPOKANE, WA 99201

ART OF THE BOOK, S.211 Howard. Deals with distributors only. Harrumph.

THE BOOK GALLERY, W. 429 First Street. Good, small, general bookstore. Wife manages but husband is boss-buyer, and scarce.

CLARK'S OLD BOOK STORE, W. 318 Sprague. Closed when I stopped by—but jammed with books, used mostly.

B. DALTON, W. 700 Riverside. The chain again, yes. The manager was out in this particular case, and while I generally drew blanks from Dalton and Walden, feedback indicates local managers can and do buy books So **work** 'em.

EREWHON, W. 605 First St. An early-on customer by mail, not open when I visited.

EPICUREAN ENTERPRISES, S. 111 Wall. Never got here—if you do let me know what the hell it is.

JOHN W. GRAHAM, W. 425 Riverside Ave. (Box 1465). See Lorraine Weigand, buyer. Big, general, excellent bookstore in a city of rather odd, half-hearted used/christian/porn shops. Has several departments, both paper and hardback stock. Pays.

GONZAGA UNIVERSITY BOOKSTORE, Boone Ave. Large store but no soul-adventure.

INLAND BOOKSTORE, W. 916 Sprague. Fair general bookstore. Boss-man splits for summer siesta so hit early in season. A prospect in a tough rivertown, at least. Paperback, new/used.

OWL'S ROOST, S. 28 Greene, Astrology.

PASTIME FEMINIST BOOK CENTER, S. 151 Lincoln. Looks good, but closed the day of our visit.

THEOSOPHICAL AND OCCULT BOOKS, E. 908 Ermina. Occult.

COEUR d'ALENE, ID 83814

THE BOOKSELLER, 206 North 4th St. Excellent place, though small and bound to be selective because of space. Very interested in independent-press publishing.

NORTH IDAHO STATE COLLEGE BOOKSTORE, 100 W. Garden Ave. Closed for inventory & resented my busting in. But generally prospective, I think.

WILSON'S PHARMACY, 403 Sherman Ave. Many books, mostly paperbacks, but still a pharmacy. Nicely rigged so you have to pass through the books to get drugs. I think we have to get into these places; a middle-Amerika hangout. Wilson bought six **Grassmans** and handed me ten bucks and some change—all in the twang of a bowstring.

MISSOULA, MT 59801

BOOK CITY, 2609 Brooks. Carries general-trade paperbacks. Buyer is at: 1928 10th Ave., great Falls, MT 59401.

BOOKS UNLIMITED, 118 W. Central Ave. A co-op? Couldn't find, but it was alleged to exist.

FREDDY'S FEED AND READ, 1221 Helen Ave. Near university, small, whole-earth, old **Directory** customer. Best prospect in town for small presses.

GARDEN CITY NEWS, 329 N. Higgins Ave. Newsstands in the sparse West are not the same as those in the East: most are really bookstores of some dimension more than NAL outlets. This one is no exception; good prospect for certain general-trade books, mags.

HAUGEN'S, HammondArcadeBldg., Higgins Ave. Good prospect all around—hardbacks, paper, mags; how-to, women, the West. Straight.

UNIVERSITY OF MONTANA BOOKSTORE. This university is in "enrollment" trouble, and the bookstore claims to sell only to students; no novels. Not interested in **Directory** or **COSMEP Catalog.**

THE OFFICE SUPPLY CO., 115 W. Broadway. Bookstore is an adjunct—and a good one—to office goods. Somewhat limited to western Americana, how-to. Owner is friendly, proud of his books.

143

DEER LODGE, MT 59722

BOOKS AND RECORDS, 306 Milwaukee Ave. Very small, but good selection and attitude in a mountain town, home of Montana State Prison.

BUTTE, MT 59701

P.O. NEWSSTAND, 43 W. Park St. This town, home of Evel Knievel, is a depressed mining city. Books are credit-card items. This particular store is good for only the most general paperbacks. Payment may be slow—I dropped six **Grassman**s just to have some in the city, but no word yet.

BOZEMAN, MT 59715

ECON-O-READ, 15 S. Tracy Ave. never found it but it's supposed to exist.

MONTANA STATE UNIVERSITY BOOKSTORE, Student Union Bldg., MSU. One of my larger sales—$50 in assorted titles plus humane treatment. Manager is Edwin Howard. This is one of the biggest bookstores we visited, with a full array of titles. It is also one of the most pleasant towns on the trail.

PHILLIPS' BOOK AND OFFICE SUPPLY, 111 E. Main St. This is Bozeman's "downtown" bookstore, about a fourth hardbacks, wide selection, good women's section and some how-to, Indian, texts. Sold both paper and cloth here, with payment.

WHITE CHAPEL BOOKS, 1528 W. Main St. So named because it's a bookstore in what once was a chapel. Christopher Harris, manager. Small-scale operation, good selection, mostly paper. No mags. Likes consignment, but paid on billing in sixty days.

LIVINGSTON, MT 59047

SAX & FREYER, W. Callendar St. A department store booksection. Western Americana/Indian, some how-to.

BIG TIMBER, MT 59011

THE BUCKSKIN PRESS, McCleod St. John Baird is the manager, publishes books on the old Hawken rifle and other materials relating to pioneer heritage and crafts. He played for me a dulcimer which he'd made himself from a piece of wood he'd brought from Indiana. Very small but fine shop. Western Americana specialist.

BILLINGS, MT 59101

HART-ALBIN BOOKSTORE, Broadway and First Ave. North. Department store. Not interested in gambling on new, unpublicized titles.

HATCH'S BOOKS, West Park Plaza. This is a good-sized, busy store—the only really general bookstore in Billings, a town of more than 60,000. Myrna Jenness, the manager, will drive a hard bargain, but you're stuck with it. Took both **Grassman** and **Directory**.

ROCKY MOUNTAIN COLLEGE BOOKSTORE, RMC. Very small college, tiny store, but manager Lois Stiffler is interested in bringing outside world in, we think.

SHERIDAN WY 82801

SHERIDAN STATIONERY CO., 206 North Main St. Small but singular. Only place in town.

BIG HORN, WY 82833

SHERIDAN COLLEGE BOOKSTORE. Very small two-year college. Bookstore manager is involved with some local writers.

BUFFALO, WY 82834

BUFFALO BULLETIN BOOKSTORE, 33 North Main Street, Box 730. Jack Williams, Mgr. Mixes stationery and books, but seems to carry good variety. In this part of the country, sparse, choices are limited. Try 'em.

CASPER, WY 82600

BAILY SCHOOL SUPPLY, 515 West Collins Drive. Children.

LANGE'S BOOKSHOP, 136 South Wolcott. Robert B. Lange. Small, but good selection from whole earth to modern poets. A sometime mail customer, of the Directory. A poet named Levendosky has influence in this store.

RALPH'S BOOKS AND CARDS, Hilltop Center. Good location in shopping center, fair selection, very general.

THE WESTERNER, 245 South Center Street. This is the largest and best prospect in Casper.

SPEARFISH, SOUTH DAKOTA 57783

SPEARFISH BOOK, 631 Main Street. New owners, receptive to new titles. This area is summer tourist-influenced, probably not very prospective after September or before June.

THE SUPPLY, Black Hills State College. Very small, but manager is forward-looking.

DEADWOOD, SD 57732

DRY GULCH ART GALLERY, Main and Lee Streets (basement). Joe Cilentic, mgr. Summer tourists. Regional selection.

LEAD, SD 57701

WESTERN DRUG, 301 West Main Street. I saw no other books in here but sold him some **Grassmans**. Maybe started something, maybe not.

RAPID CITY, SD 55701

CLEARING HOUSE FOR MIND AND MEDIA 515 Main Street. Very interested in small presses but not much money. Just getting started.

HALLMARK, St. Joseph & 7th. Mostly cards, some books.

PAUPER'S BOOKSTORE, 201 Main Street. New bookstore. Good general but small selection.

WESTERN STATIONERS, P.O. Box 1152, 711 St. Joseph St. Quite large, and straight. Fair prospect for any general trade title.

WALL, SD 57790

WALL DRUG. This is a great circus of a smudge on the Dakota plains, a kind of rambling mall in the middle of nowhere Encloses at least bookstore, caters to summer traffic. Books are ordered in winter.

SIOUX FALLS, SD 57100

AUGUSTANA COLLEGE BOOKSTORE, Morrison Commons Bldg. Lloyd Frick, Mgr. Small store, conservative manager, but did stock some Directories and a couple of the novel.

BOOK GALLERY, Western Mall. Small store, manager hard to find. General selection.

COLLEGE STORE, Sioux Falls College. Manager signs herself Mrs. Howard Eager. Seems reasonably adventuresome and has good variety for a small store.

COURTNEY'S BOOKS AND THINGS, 2119 South Minnesota. Mrs. Anderson, Mgr. To some extent things rather than books.

DAKOTA NEWS AGENCY, 828 North Main

Street. A wholesaler, taking 47% discount and consignment. A last resort here.

B. DALTON, Western Mall. Latest feedback and experience on Dalton: If author is local, individual store will order. Otherwise write to 9340 James Ave. S, Minneapolis, MN 55435, c/o Joni Miller, hardcover, John Schultz, paperback.

READER'S DEN, 107 South Phillips. Small, all ordering is through Dakota News Agency (above).

FAIRMONT, MINNESOTA 56031

NEWS BOOKSTORE, 114 East 3rd Street. General, busy, good prospect.

ALBERT LEA, MN 56007

BROADWAY BOOKSTORE, 346 S. Broadway

FEATURE OFFICE SERVICES, 136 S. Newton.

AUSTIN, MN 55912

NEIMITZ BOOK AND TOBACCO, 415 N. Main.

LA CROSSE, WISCONSIN 54601

BEST BUYS, 216 South 3rd St. In a tough area of town; some borderline porn. Limited possibilities for certain mags.

BOOK EXCHANGE, State Street between 3rd and 4th. Open half day, many used, some rare books, few new.

HONIG'S GIFT AND BOOK SHOP, 531 Main St. A downtown, middle-road shop, general trade.

McKAY'S TOWN/CAMPUS BOOKSTORE, 1908 Campbell Road. Across from university (of Wisconsin-LaCrosse). Excellent variety, student-oriented, interest in small presses and publishing in general.

READMORE, 125 North 7th. "The only thing I have to recommend this book is your presence. Why should I buy it?" "It might sell....?"."You're from California?" "Yes." "Well, everyone has his problems...." Blmphhh.

UNIVERSITY BOOKSTORE, University of Wisconsin-LaCrosse. Manager is Peter Brunner who knows Mangelsdorff and others on the Madison-Milwaukee scene. Store is next to cafeteria, small but lively. Brunner is interested in small presses, limited, probably, by space.

VITERBO COLLEGE, 9th and Winnebago. Stopped cold by someone at desk who would not say what kind of college this was, nor reveal location of bookstore.

MADISON, WI 53700

ART MART, 8 South Carroll. Only art books will go here.

BRATHE'S BOOKSTORE, 665 University Avenue. Were having a close-out sale, so, depending on what that meant, may be closed by now.

BROWN'S BOOKSTORE, 673 State Street. Ideal location next to University. Huge store with great variety from women-whole earth-energy to texts. Manager is a little cautious in ordering, likes to play golf, but is amiable and knowledgeable.

LABOR BOOK CENTER, 409 North Frances.

LADY CYBELE'S CAULDRON, 405 West Gilman. Didn't get here—if you do let me know what it is.

MICROCOSM BOOKSTORE, 306 West Lakeside.

MOSELEY'S INC., 24 East Mifflin. A mail-order house and retail store. Over the years I have dealt with them by mail, and they seem genuinely (if not heavily) interested in small-press materials. At this point, though, in keeping with the rest of 4:30 Madison, reasonable barter could not prevail.

NELSON'S BOOKS AND STATIONERY, 3238 University Avenue. This is in a small shopping center and is reasonably up-to-date. Unable to sell westerns, she said, and stuck with that attitude through all the other titles I then presented. Should be a fair bet though, if you, as they say, engender positive reactions at the outset.

PAUL'S, 670 State Street. Deals with distributors, not publishers.

PIC-A-BOOK STORE, 506 State Street. Big store, much variety, much used, etc. The guy wanted consignment, but it was hot, humid and hungry out in Madison (& I needed some gas money) so I hesitated on that. He turned himself off, saying "I've been burned before."

SAKTI BOOK SHOP, 320 State Street. Yoga and metaphysical.

UNIVERSITY BOOKSTORE, 711 State Street. Massive and impersonal, at least three floors of books. You find the p'back buyer on the third floor, and once you do **that** the hard part is over.

WALDEN BOOKS, 46 East Towne Mall. See main man in Connecticut, etc.

ZONDERVAN FAMILY BOOKSTORE, 174 East Towne Mall. "Family" in this business often connotes juvenile and/or religious books. Up-down stare at travel-worn clothes.

MADISON WHOLESALERS:

INTERSTATE PERIODICAL DISTRIBUTORS INC., 201 East Badger road.

WISCONSIN INDEPENDENT NEWS DEPT., 811½ Williamson. This was recommended as an "alternative" distributor, but we couldn't locate it.

SOUTH BEND/MISHAWAKA, INDIANA 46540

AQUINAS BOOKSTORE, 18717 Bulla Road. Small, limited, Catholic (near Notre Dame Campus) but rather open in certain attitudes.

BETHEL CAMPUS STORE, Mishawaka. Very small—too small, but a good source of info about writers groups.

BOOK SHACK, 2340 Miracle Lane, Mishawaka. Took five books and squeezed me for a 45% discount. "People expect a cut rate in here."

BOOKWORLD, 111 Lincoln Way East, Mishawaka. Retail/wholesale chain; central ordering through MAJEREK'S, Althea Adkins, Niles, Michigan (just across the Indiana border north).

BRUGGNER'S TOWN AND COUNTRY, 3520 Miracle Lane, Mishawaka. Shopping center, general trade.

COMMUNITY NEWS STAND, 113 West Monroe. In center of South Bend, tough but friendly place. Buys through The Distributor (see next).

THE DISTRIBUTOR, 1635 North Ironwood, South Bend 46635. A new, "alternative" distributor covering a large portion of the midwest. Run by four people (Steve, Kathy, Ray, Marilyn) out of a huge, cool basement warehouse. Friendly, competent and eager to know about new small-press titles.

MODERN AGE BOOKSTORE, 327 West 7th, Mishawaka. Small, occult.

WALDEN BOOKS, 1246 Scottsdale Mall.

ZONDERVAN FAMILY BOOKSTORE, 1130 Scottsdale Mall. Mainstream children's titles might appeal to this chain.

MIDDLETOWN, NEW YORK 10940

BROWSE HOUSE. We lost the address for this store. Looked like a fair prospect for some small-press titles. If anyone lives in the area of Port Jervis-Middletown, maybe they could send in address?

OUR PLACE, 19 West Main Street. Good, hip bookstore with many non-big-publisher titles. At time of my visit they had a roof leaking, but I presume that is fixed.

STORRS, CONNECTICUT, 06268

FOLLETTS UNIV OF CONN BOOKSTORE #392, University of Connecticut. Mostly interested in non-fiction titles.

WILLIMANTIC, CT 06226

BOOK EMPORIUM, 768 Main Street. Name is misleading—it is **not** a supermarket but a fine and knowing store.

WESTFIELD, MASSACHUSETTS 01085

LARKIN'S BOOKSTORE, 191 East Main Street. A general-title store in a small shopping plaza, but better than most of its kind.

SPRINGFIELD, MA 01003

BOOK HAVEN, Main Street. Good location, variety, but skeptical of non-ordinary.

JOHNSON'S BOOKSTORE, Main Street.

Somewhat conservative, but wide variety and number of titles.

THE JOURNAL, 93 State Street. Joe Marino, Prop. Very small store—but if he likes your stuff he'll buy and pay.

PAPERBACK BOOKSMITH, 1570 Boston Road. Shopping mall store.

WALDEN BOOKS, 1055 Boston Road. By this time you're near enough to the main office in Stamford, Conn. to go **there** and save some futility.

MANCHESTER, NEW HAMPSHIRE 03100

BOOK BAZAAR, 18 Hanover Street. In the West the word **bazaar** (which in the East means a market for fine goods) usually denotes a flea market....

BOOK GALLERY, Zayre Shopping Center, 611 Elm Street. Buys through Manchester News Company (see below).

GOODMAN'S, 809 Elm Street. Main downtown store, probably best bet in this dark old Mill Town.

LAURIAT'S, Hampshire Plaza (Elm Street). Orders centrally, but the manager, Barbara Wall (Merrimack Road, Amherst, NH 03031) bought a personal **Whole Cosmep Catalog**.

MANCHESTER BOOK MART, 1173 Elm Street. No boss, only fair prospect.

TWO WORLDS BOOK SHOPPE, 27 Elm Street. Occult & cordial.

BEDFORD, NH 03102

MANCHESTER NEWS COMPANY, 10 Roundlett Hill Road. Mainly, of course, a mass-market distributor of mags and paperbacks. Worth a flyer. **Not** worth trying to find unless you know the territory.

YORK BEACH, ME 03910

PAPERBACK BOOKSMITH, Bedford Mall. Took some novels on consignment. Paperback Booksmith is an east coast chain of plaza shops "dedicated to the fine art of browsing." Stores appear to have home rule, however, unlike Walden/Dalton.

GARFIELD'S. Small but centrally located store. Sells newspapers by the ton. Viable only in the summer for general trade.

OGUNQUIT, MAINE 03907

THE COVE BOOKSTORE, 5 Oarweed Lane (Box 515). Very small and artsy. Novelty items will go here. Manager reluctantly took two **Grassman**s on consignment—and sold them.

KENNEBUNKPORT, ME 04046

KENNEBUNKPORT BOOK, Port Square. This somewhat artsy store is on second floor at east side of the small square. We parried book knowledge for a bit, he brandishing LMP and BIP, I the Directory and **Small Press Record**. He won in the good old American capital tradition—it was his store. Less than a mile from where I started in newspapers in '57.

PORTLAND, ME 04100

CONGRESS BOOK SHOP, 668 Congress Street. Seventy-five percent porn, and an honest manager: "We do a hundred a week out front" (non-porn) and a thousand a week out back" (porn). "What can I say?"

EASTERN BOOK COMPANY, 131 Middle Street. See Dan McDonough. This is a jobber/distributor which every small press should be listed with.

JONES BOOK SHOP, 611 Congress Street. **Grassman** blurb says the author "feels uncomfortable east of the Mississippi" and the two operators here decided to take that personally. At this point this fatsouled, vorpal town began to edge me as it had when I lived in a dank tenement on Park Street in the mid-fifties.

PAPERBACK BOOK MART, 469 Congress Street. If books were horses Portland would walk.

PORTLAND NEWS COMPANY, 270 Western Ave., South Portland. Local distributor—has my sympathy.

UNIVERSITY OF MAINE AT PORTLAND-GORHAM, 96 Falmouth Street. Assistant manager took 3 directories and 4 novels. The books were waiting when I got back to California, so apparently big boss bitched. So much for the old Alma Mater.

FALMOUTH, ME 04105

BOOK AND YARN BARN, Falmouth Shopping Center. Craft and children's books.

KNUDSEN'S GIFT SHOP, Falmouth Shoppinh Center. 'speciality and gift books, Gibran, etc.

THE NORTH NODE BOOKSTORE, Falmouth Shopping Center. A new store with much promise. General trade, women, children's books.

MONTPELIER, VERMONT 05602

BEAR POND BOOKS, 100 Main Street. A surprisingly nice find in a mid-mountain town, Took **Cosmep Catalog, Directories, Grassman**. Holds promise for small presses.

BURLINGTON, VT 05401

BURLINGTON NEWS AGENCY, 266 South Champlain. Wholesale distributor.

CITY BOOKSTORE, INC., 1301 Williston Road, So. Burlington.

CORNER BOOKSTORE, 117 Church St. Two or three floors of books, all manner of titles. Took **Grassman** (5), sold 2 and returned 3 in six months.

EVERYDAY BOOKSHOP, 106 church Street. Small. Had **The Domebuilder's Handbook** (Running Press) and **The Ten Week Garden** (Something Else Press) but would **not** speculate on **The Grassman**.

THE LITTLE PROFESSOR BOOKCENTER, 40 Church Street. Tinker Greene, Mgr. and poet. This is a nationwide chain of stores, usually in shopping malls or near universities. We had good luck all the way from Burlington to Reno with these—but I've been unable to acquire a masterlist of them. Any help?

UNIVERSITY STORE, University of Vermont. Worth a try. We sold some Directories.

WHY NOT R.E.A.D., Ethan Allen Shopping Center, North Avenue. Didnt make it here, but the name pulls.

OTHER MID-VERMONT POSSIBILITIES:

VERMONT BOOKSHOP, 38 Main St., Middlebury 05753. Breadloaf is here, e.g.

BEAR POND BOOKS, Lenox Village, Stowe 05672. Kin to the Montpelier shop. If books are no go there's a health-food restaurant next door that'll treat you right.

BRATTLEBORO, VT 05301

THE BOOK CELLAR, 120 Main Street. Took some books and shows promise.

BAKER'S BOOKSTORE, Main Street. Mrs. Bracke. Couldn't find her. Store is a Hallmark outlet.

KEENE, NH 03431

MANDALA, 38 Washington Street. John and Jay Crystal. Both were out when I visited, which was my loss because store is a small-press **place**.

TILDEN'S, 55 Main Street. Big, general trade store with a sharp book manager. I lived just outside Keene when the '38 hurricane blew the town flat (I was four and so possess only a reference in trauma for it.) Mention that here and you're off on right foot.

SYRACUSE, NY 13200

THE BOOK HOUSE, Shop City Shopping Center. Never found this.

CHASE'S CIGAR STORE, 2823 James. Small selection of popular paperbacks. Not a good bet.

ECONOMY BOOK AND STATIONARY STORE, 317 South Salina Street. See Jerry Brock, the book buyer. Big downtown store, open to ideas and new possibilities.

FAIRMOUNT BOOKS, Fairmount Shopping Center. Looked good from the outside but slammed a flat **no** down on all titles.

LOGOS BOOKSTORE, Waverly Street. The Waverly-Marshall Street confluence here is to Syracuse as Telegraph is to Berkeley and State is to Madison. Generally novels are harder to place than other books (except maybe poetry). Here, the prop. looked up two private presses of her knowledge in the Directory and, not finding them, shuffled me on out.

ONONDAGA NEWS AGENCY, 628 Montgomery. Local distributor.

SYRACUSE BOOK CENTER, 113 Marshall Street. Achilles Nichols, prop. Walt Sheppard, Joe Bruchac and I set up shop along the sidewalk fronting this store and sold some books. Store is old mail customer with Dustbooks. Small but very sensitive to small presses.

SYRACUSE UNIVERSITY BOOKSTORE, First, the place was impossible to find and we got lost in the great dark and empty student union; second, the child-buyer wanted 40% on two Directories while putting down the small presses; third, I held to the official discount (25% on 2—5 copies) as moods darkened; fourth, while we haggled over pennies, I spotted a carton of Jacqueline Suzanne's latest and so, fifth, walked out. One of my few stomp-aways in 25 dozen stores.

BUFFALO, NY 14200

NOTE: Bad planning here. We struck town just after 3 PM and became imprisoned in a bathroomless, **mapless** downtown mall. By the time we broke free we could only visit a half-dozen stores. Hence, the annotations are limited. Buffalo is a **great** book town, though, and people like Creely, DeLoach and others have done their homework with booksellers.

ABC BOOKSTORE, 112 Genesee (near East Chippewa).

BOOK ART, 4 East Chippewa.

BOOK MART, 610 Main Street.

BOOK SALES STORE, 628 Main Street.

BOOKS INTERNATIONAL, 626 Main Street.

BUFFALO TEXTBOOK STORES, 3610 Main Street.

EVERYMAN'S BOOKSTORES, 3102 Main Street. A small store, but one which knows the Buffalo small press scene.

GRANT BOOK AND STAMP, 1122 Elmwood.

LIBBY'S BOOKSTORE, 728 Main Street.

THE LITTLE PROFESSOR BOOKCENTER, University Plaza, 3500 Main street. Melissa

Kidd, prop. Another good store in this chain.

MAIN STREET BOOKSTORE, 659 Main Street.

PEOPLE'S BOOKSTORE, 1526 Main Street. Third world.

SUNY-BUFFALO BOOKSTORE, 3435 Main Street. It closed, very nearly on my fingers, but looks like a good bet.

ULBRICH'S, 446 Main Street. Paperback buyer is William Mailia. This is a big downtown department **book** store. Mailia asked me who were the major literary influences on **The Grassman**. I said Manfred, Clark, Wister, Doby. He ordered 25.

WALDEN BOOKS, Main Plaza Mall, and Seneca Mall (W. Seneca).

WESTSIDE BOOKS, 17 West Chippewa.

YOUTHTIME SWORD AND SHIELD BOOKSTORE, 512 Pearl Street.

PITTSBURGH, PENNSYLVANIA 15200

NOTE: The job here was bigger than the time we had for it. We spent two fine days as guests of Anne Pride (KNOW) and her husband Ed, spent the first day selling books and the second promoting them. Pittsburgh is huge, quaint, conjested, and you need two full days on the street to cover all bases.

AMERICAN HORSE, 119 Meyran Avenue. An old mail customer and small press bookstore. Good bet.

BEECHVIEW NEWS, 1544 Beechview Ave.

BELLEVUE BOOK & RECORD SHOP, 616 Lincoln Ave.

BLOCKS BOOKSHOP, 339 Butler, Etna.

BOOK MARK INC., 703 Washington Road.

COKESBURY, 9th and Penn Avenue. Nice store but not a place for small presses or experiments in either capital enterprise or literature.

FAMILY BOOKSTORE, South Hills Village Shopping Center.

GIMBEL'S, 5th Avenue. Books are on 6th floor of this huge department store. I feel these are generally good possibilities for small presses.

JAY'S BOOK STALL, 3604 5th Avenue.

KAUFMANN'S, 5th Avenue and Smithfield (400 5th). Department #42 is books. Manager of the department knows novels **and** something of small presses.

MATHEW BENDEN & CO., Park Bldg.

NATIONAL RECORD MART (D. Fine), 230 Forbes Avenue. "Mart" in American capital English is a little like "bazaar"—it possesses a certain meaning in madness. Here you have a supermarket for records and books with five P'burgh locations.

RANDALL'S, S.W. 1706 Sahdy Avenue.

SIGN OF AQUARIUS, 815 Copeland. Occult.

F.W. SKELDER, 240 Forbes Avenue. Many used books, somewhat disorganized.

UNIVERSITY OF PITTSBURGH BOOK CENTER, 5th Avenue and Bigelow (4000 5th). Good reception here, and big sale. Knows books, aware of need to know about small presses.

WESTERN DISTRIBUTING CO., 4650 Friendship Avenue. Wholesaler.

COLUMBUS, OHIO 43200

NOTE: This was a beastly Saturday punctuated by unrelenting Ohio heat, a busted California car, and a week's-end blues. So:

BOOKSTORE, 19 East Town Avenue.

CATHEDRAL BOOK SHOP, 224 East Broadway.

COLUMBUS WHOLESALE BOOK CO., 1391 Oakland Park. Wholesaler.

GERMAN VILLAGE, 555 City Park.

GOOD BOOK STORES, Westland Shopping Center, and 4225 Shoppers Lane.

LION'S DEN, 4309 Westerville.

LITTLE PROFESSOR BOOK CENTER, 1660 Neil Avenue. Mgr. not in Saturday. Central address for this chain is 33200 Capital, Livonia, Michigan 48150.

LOGOS BOOKSHOP, 1764 N. High Street. Ken Palmer, bookbuyer.

LONG'S, 1836 N. High Street. A flat **no.**

PAPERBOOK GALLERY, 147 N. High Street. A **no.**

PHOENIX BOOKS LTD., 295 Brehl.

READ-MOR, 131 N. High Street. Couldn't locate manager.

SCOTT KRAUS NEWS AGENCY, 777 Goodale. Wholesalers.

VINEYARD, 2766 W. Broad Street.

WORLDWIDE, 3608 W. Broad Street.

CHAMPAIGN-URBANA, ILLINOIS 61820

BOOK CENTER, The Illini Union, Urbana. Jim Anderson, buyer. Looks like a good bet if you can find the man.

BOOK EMPORIUM, Coventry Fair Shopping Center, Champaign.

BOOK EXCHANGE, 301½ 51, Champaign. Father-daughter management. Very small store. Interested in horses.

BOOK NOOK, 501 N. Neil, Champaign. Why is porn sold by the humorless??

THE CARD SHOP, 125 W. Park Avenue, Champaign. See Pat Wolfinbarger, Mgr.

CARSON PIRIE SCOTT, Lincoln Square Center, Urbana.

ELYSIAN TREE METAPHYSICAL STORE, 122 W. Main Street, Champaign. Closed at this point, but try it if it's in your line of vision.

FOLLET'S U OF I BOOK AND SUPPLY, Store #221, 627-631 S. Wright Street, Champaign. Largest store in town. Stocked both Directory and **Grassman**.

MY FAVORITE THINGS, 907 Lincoln Square Center, Urbana.

ROBESON'S DEPARTMENT STORE, 125 W. Church Street, Champaign. Mgr. just off vacation and ordering all books through Doubleday to save time. I think in calmer moments she'd be interested in broader view.

THE USED BOOKSTORE, 1001 S. Wright Street, Champaign (in basement of YMCA Bldg.). Used, yes. but bought a Directory and seemed interested in small presses.

IOWA CITY, IOWA 52240

DRUM C. BOOKSELLERS, 5 Paul Helen Bldg.

EPSTEIN'S, ABC Clinton Mall. A rather immediate and unequivocal **no**.

IOWA BOOK AND SUPPLY CO., 8 S. Clinton. Took 5 Directories. Only real show in this town. You expect more—but it ain't there.

UNIVERSITY OF IOWA BOOKSTORE, Madison and Jefferson Streets. Closed at this point (July 30th) for summer and inventory.

WAYNE'S BOOKSHOP, 114 E. Washington. Gifts and children's books.

DES MOINES, IA 50310

THE BOOKSTORE, 901 Locust. No Sale. This is the big downtown store, but is adventurless.

COKESBURY, 3839 Merle Hay Road.

HYMAN'S, 9th and Locust. Mags, mostly slicks.

LAMPLIGHTER, 415 Euclid. Largely used, low-key—but only store in this town to buy a **Grassman**.

TONY'S BOOKSTORE, 545 5th Avenue.

THE UNIVERSITY BOOKSTORE, 1213 25th Street. No connection to Drake University which is across the street and has **no** bookstore. This one would hardly seem to suffice.

OMAHA, NEBRASKA 68100

ANTIQUARIAN BOOKSTORE, 1210 Farnum. Judy S. Rudloff, Mgr. Mostly used, but nice folks and did buy a Directory and a novel.

BELLEVUE BOOKSHOP, Wright Way at Galvin Road S.

CITY NEWS AND BOOK CO., 412 S. 16th. Wholesaler.

ELYSIAN FIELDS, 423 S. 11th. Mgr. was out, but this looked to be a fair prospect down in the reclaimed stockyard area.

MATHEWS BOOKSTORE, 1620 Harvey. Claimed doesn't do well with novels.

NELSON NEWS INC., 4651 F. Wholesaler.

READING RACK, 280 Alpine Mall, Westroads. A great cavernous mall. The bookstore is buried within and the attendant dosen't make decisions on stock by himself.

VILLAGE BOOK SHOP, 87 and Pacific.

UNIVERSITY OF NEBRASKA AT OMAHA BOOKSTORE, 60th & Dodge Street. Ben Koenig is the manager and bought ten Directories. He owns 20 acres over near Council Bluffs, Iowa, and loves to talk about wildlife.

LINCOLN, NE 68500

CAMPUS BOOK STORE, 1245 R Street. Mostly textbooks & trinkets.

CITY NEWS AND BOOK CO., 412 S. 16th Street. Wholesaler.

LOGOS BOOKSTORE, 204 N. 13th Street. Many religious books. Looked through **Grassman** and decided no.

MILLER & PAINE, 13th & O Street. Downtown department store with books on back end. Talked me out of a Grassman to show buyers later and that's the last I heard of it.

NEBRASKA BOOKSTORE, 1135 R Street. Mgr. not in. Looks like maybe **the** place in this hot, hard town, if any.

PLAINSMAN BOOKSTORE, Nebraska Wesleyan University Bookstore. Closed up for summer.

CHEYENNE, WYOMING 82001

CITY NEWS, 1722 Carey Avenue. All books through distributor: Bud Carlson, Poudre Valley News, 603 Lesson Drive, Ft. Collins, CO 80521.

HATCH'S BOOK STORE #53, 303 Cole Shopping Center. Good store and good folks. Probably room here for progress.

SHAFER'S BOOKSTORE, 104 W. 17th. "Cheyenne's complete bookstore," it says. Downtown, carries art supplies. Buys modestly, but buys.

LARAMIE, WY 82070

BOOKS A GO GO, 408 University Avenue (P.O. Box 670). This is **the** non-campus store, downtown. Good selection, plenty room for more. If you have any western Americana....

WEST BOOK STORE, 506 S. 21st. Another argument about BIP, this time in a hodgepodge place.

UNIVERSITY OF WYOMING BOOKSTORE, P.O. Box 3255 Univ. Sta. Another Alma Mater here, so took some books. The small press people in Laramie have probably opened some heads.

SALT LAKE CITY, UTAH 84100

BEEHIVE SPECIALTY FOODS, 191 W. 2100 S.

BLUE DRUID, 325 S. State. Astrology.

BONNEVILLE NEWS CO., 965 Beardsley Place. Wholesaler.

BOOK CRAFT, 1848 W. 2100 S.

BY'S MAGAZINE SHOP, 228 S. Main. Mean.

CARR STATIONERY, 185 S, Main.

CENTRAL BOOK EXCHANGE, 2017 S. 1100 E.

COTTONWOOD BOOKS, Cottonwood Mall, 4835 Highland Drive.

DESERET BOOKSTORE, 60 E. South Temple (offices at 1610 Empire Road). Big place. I visited with buyer who promised to order but never did.

DICK'S BOOK EXCHANGE, 3221 W. 3500.

FROST'S BOOK AND RECORD, 3977 Wasatch Blvd. (also 1320 Foothill Drive).

GREAT BOOKS OF THE WESTERN WORLD, 2343 E. 3300 S.

QUALITY BOOKSTORE, 71 W. 300 S. Used, rare.

UNIVERSITY BOOKSTORE, University of Utah Campus. Lester A. Perry, buyer. Stocked Directories.

UTAH COLLEGE BOOKSTORE, 200 University Street. G.S. Wood, Mgr. Stocked both **Grassman** and Directory. Good selection and variety, though not a large store.

RENO, NEVADA 89500

ZION BOOKSTORE, 254 S. Main Street. Large store in center of downtown action. Super western collection.

BAKER & TAYLOR CO., 380 Edison Way. This is the western branch of one of the largest and, for the small presses, most promising nationwide book distributors.

BOOKS'N TIQUES, 257 E. Plum Lane.

LITTLE PROFESSOR BOOK CENTER, 949 W. Moana. This is about as far west as they get—but still good for a sale.

PAPERBACK EXCHANGE, 304 Vassar. Almost all used.

UNIQUE BOOK STALL, 448 N. Virginia. Probably best bet in town for the small presses. Directory was already in stock. Carries only "Nevada" fiction, whatever that is.

R.S. DISTRIBUTORS, 21 locust. Wholesaler.

TAHOE CITY, CA 95730

THE TIDES, 195 River Road. Touristy but nicely located where roads converge north-south around Lake Tahoe. May go in small quantities for gift-like items. Stocked both Directory and novel.

Subject Index

Agawam, 19, 20, 78
Airstream Trailers, Convention of, 62
Albany (Oregon), 29
Albany County Librarian, 119
Alternative Press, 27
Alternatives in Print, 26
American Library Association, 14
Arentz, 80
Argus-Leader, 55
Ashland, 27-28
Ashland Shakespeare Festival, 27
Aspects, 26
Baird, John, 37-38
Bad Lands Wall, 54
Badlands, 54
Bakken, Dick, 25
Banks, Dennis and Means, Russel, 52, 53
Barth, 94
Bass, Sam, 52
Bayes, Ron, 26
Bean, L.L., 82
Belle Fourche, 51-52
Bellows Falls, 85
Berge, Carol, 43-44
Berlin, 82
Berry, Don, 25
Big Timber, 16, 37
Billings, 17, 37
Black Hills, 52
Black Hills State College, 51
Blazek, Douglas, 36
Blitz, 26
Bonneville Salt Flats, 120
Books in Print, 26, 27, 109
Bowker, R.R., 26
Bozeman, 17, 37, 80
Brand, Stewart, 37
Brezhnev, 36
Brock, Jerry, 91
Brockman, John, 70
Bruchac, Joe, 20, 91
Brunner, Peter, 59, 60
Buckskin Press, 37
Buckskin Report, The, 37
Buffalo, 17, 18, 44, 92-94
Buffington, Mel, 26
Burlington, 83-84
Burlington Free Press, 84
Burns, Jerry, 111
Butte, 17, 37, 53

Calamity Jane, 52
California, 13,17, 25-27
Calgary, 117
Cambridge Junction, 84
Campbell County, 43, 45
Casper, 43, 45

Casper Star Tribune, 45
Center, 43
Champaign, 108
Champaign-Urbana News Gazette, 108
Cheyenne, 117
Chicago, 61, 62
Christensen, Marty, 25
Cider Press, 107
Circleville, 63
Clark, 93
Coeur d'Alene, 16, 37
Cohen, Marty, 25
Columbus, 18, 61, 107
Congdon, Kirby, 94
Conjuring A Counter-Culture, 81
Connecticut, 77, 119
Corvallis, 16, 29
COSMEP (See also Whole COSMEP Catalog, COSMEP Conference), 13, 60, 70, 71, 94, 102
COSMEP Conference:
  New York, 14-16, 71-72
  Madison, 60
  Buffalo, 92, 93
  Ann Arbor, 110-111
COSMEP-ALA Bookfair, (see New York Bookfair)
Council Bluffs, 110
Cramer, Rodger, 108
Creeley, 94
Curry, Andrew, 14
Curtis, Walt, 25
Custer Battlefield, 38-39

Daily News, 78
The Dalles, 29, 35
Danville, 82
Dark Other Adam Dreaming, 77, 85
Deadwood, 52, 53
DeLoach, Allen, 92, 93, 94
Des Moines, 17, 109
Detro, Gene, 19, 25
Detroit, 62
Dobie, 93
Dorman, Dan, 107
Doubleday, 70
Drake University, 109

East Towne Mall, 61
Ed (Kurlfink), 20, 102
Edelson, Morris, 59, 60
Edition des Femmes, 72
Elder, Gary, 26
Elko, 120
Essex, 84
Essex Junction, 84
Eubanks, Jackie, 14, 69
Eugene, 25, 28-29
Evanston, 119

Falmouth, 82
Fay, Bob, 79, 82
Fiedler, 94
Foreman, Paul, 14, 16

Fort Madison, 109
Fox, Hugh, 72
Franklin Pierce College, Rindge, 85
Frazier, Jack, 72
Freeport, 82
Freeport Press, 82

Gale, Vi, 25
Gardner, Joann, 102
Gary, 61
Gentry, Curt, 44
Gillette, 44
Glide, 26
Ginsberg, 94
Goliards, 111
Gorham, 82
Grande Ronde Review, 26
Green, Tinker, 84
Greenfield Review, 91
Grey, Zane, 43

Haas, Victor, 110
Hartford, 17, 77
Hawthorne, 77
Henderson, Nancy, 71
Henderson, William, 71
Hiatt, Ben, 26
Hickock, William (Wild Bill), 52
Huntington Hartford Museum/New York Cultural Center, 69, 71, 72

Idaho, 37
Illinois, 119
Indianapolis, 108
International Directory of Little Magazines and Small Presses, 13, 15, 18, 19, 26, 28, 29, 36, 78, 92, 102, 109, 118
Interracial Books for Children, Council of, 69
Intrepid, 92
Iowa City, 17, 109

Jackson County Library, 28
Jaques, John, 81
Jeffersonville, 84
Jericho, 84
Johnson County, 43, 44
Johnson, Curt, 82

Keene, 85
Kelso, Red, 117
Kennebunkport, 79, 82
Kennedy, Jackie, 78
Kennedy, John, 78
Kennewick, 35
Kepley, Jan, 26
Kesey, Ken, 25
Kittery, 79
KNOW Inc., 20, 99, 102
Koenig, Ben, 110
Kois, John, 59

LaCrosse, 18, 59-60
La Faye's Brindavan, 29-30
LaMoille, 77

Lancaster, 82
Laramie, 118
Lead, 52-53
Lenin, 36
Lifshin, Lyn, 36, 71
Lincoln, 17, 110
Lisbon, 82
Lisbon Enterprise, 82
Litmus, 26
Loeb, William, 78
Longfellow, 77, 79
Lowell, 79
Luschei, Glenna, 60

Mad Virgin, 26
Madison, 18, 59, 60-61
Maine, 119
Maine Sunday Telegram, 81
Maine, University of, Portland, 81
Malia, William, 93
Manchester (New Hampshire), 78, 79
Manderson, 54
Manfred, 93
Mangelsdorff, Rich. 59
Marie Torre Show, 101
Marjorie, 25
Mattingly, George, 60
Mayakovsky, 36
McCall, Jack, 52
McDonough, Dan, 81
McQuade, Joe, 78
Medford, 28
Michelson, Peter, 118
Middletown (N.Y.), 17, 62-63
Middletown Daily Record, 62
Midwest (Wyoming), 45
Milwaukee, 59
Minneapolis, 15
Mishawaka, 61
Missoula, 17, 37
Montana, 17, 37-39
Montpelier, 16, 83
Monroeville, 100
Morey, Frederick, 71, 72
Moroni, 119
Morris, Richard, 52, 60, 71, 94, 111
Mount Rushmore, 53

Nebraska, 110, 111
Nebraska Wesleyan University, 110
Nebraska-Omaha, University of, Bookstore, 110
Nebraska City, 109
Nevada, 119
New England, 77
New York Bookfair, 14, 16, 63, 69-72, 93, 102
New York City, 14, 16, 51, 63, 69
News Advertiser, 78
Niagara Falls, 94
Niles, 61
Ninety-eighth Meridian, 59, 63, 109
Nobody's Perfect, 82
Normal, 108
North Platte, 110, 111

Norton, W.W., 44
Norway, 82
Notre Dame, University of, 62
Oakmont, 99, 100
Ohio, 107
Ohio State University, 108
Omaha, 17, 109-110
Oregon, 13, 25-35, 119
Oregon Journal, 19
Ortega Y Gassett, Jose, 118
Paris, 82
Pasco, 35
Pendleton, 117
Pennsylavania, 59, 61, 62, 99, 100
Perry, Lester, 119
Phaneuff, Wayne, 78
Pine Ridge, 54
Pittsburgh, 17, 20, 99, 101-102
Pittsburgh, University of, Bookstore, 102
Pliego, 26
Poetry of Pop, The, 91
Pollack, Felix, 60
Porcupine, 54
Port Jervis, 62
Portland (Maine), 20, 61, 80-81
Portland (Oregon), 25, 29
Portland Poetry Festival, 26
Post, The New York, 71
Potato Creek, 54
Potts, Charles, 26
Press Herald, 81
Pride, Anne, 20, 72, 99, 101, 102
Publish it Yourself Handbook, The, 71
Pyros, John, 94
Quixote, 60
Randolph, 82
Rapid City, 18, 53
Red Bluff, 15, 26
Redding, 26
Reyes, Carlos 26
Ribar, (Buffalo) Joe, 27, 71
Richland, 35
Roberts, Kenneth, 80
Robertson, Foster, 71
Salem, 25, 29
Salt Lake, 120
Salt Lake City, 119
Schneider, Bob, 108
Seattle, 26
Second Coming, 108
7 On Style, 108
Seventeen, 71
Shameless Hussy Press, 71
Shepperd, Walt, 20, 91
Sheridan County, 43
Silberman, Jim, 37
Simmons, Ralph, 94
Simpson, Jerry Paul, 26
Sioux Falls, 16, 54-55
Skratz, G.P., 27
Small Press Record of Books, 26
Small Press Review, 70
Smith, Harry, 71

Smuggler's Notch, 85
Source, The, 108
South Bend, 61-62
South Dakota, 51-55, 119
Spearfish, 51
Spokane (Expo '74), 16, 35-37
Springfield (Massachusetts), 78
Stamford, 15
Steinbeck, John, 19
Stock Growers Association, 117
Stone Press Weekly, 27
Stowe, 85
Sturgis, 51, 52, 63
Sudbury, 83
Suzanne, Jacqueline, 92
Swallow, Alan, 44
Syracuse, 17, 20, 91-92
Tahoe City, 15
Teapot Dome, 45
Thoreau, 77
Thorp Springs Press, 13, 14, 44, 70
Three Rivers Press, 101
Thunder Basin, 16, 43, 45, 80
Times, The New York, 71, 78
Times-Herald, 62
Times-Herald-Record, 62
Tourist Topic, 79
Underhill, 84
Union Leader, 78
Vermont, 77
Vermont, University of, 84
Vonbruns, Barbara, 84
Wall, 54
Wall Drug, 53-54
Wantling, Ruthie, 108
Wantling, William, 36, 60, 91, 108
Washington, 13, 35-37
Weekly News, 82
Welburn, Ron, 91
Wells, 120
Wheelan, Joe, 45
Wieners, 94
Winnemucca, 120
Wister, 93
Whole COSMEP Catalog, 13, 15, 36, 44, 69, 70, 71, 102
Whole Earth Catalog, 37
Wilde, Ina, 72
Wisconsin, 59-61
Wisconsin, University of, Library, 60
World Herald (omaha), 78, 110
Wounded Knee, 54
Wyoming, 16, 43-45, 118, 119
Wyoming Eagle, 117
Wyoming, University of, 118
Yevtushenko, 38
Yreka, 27
Zaddock, Bob and Jean, 28

Index to Bookstores

ABC Bookstore, 158
Richard Abel, 81
Alternative, The, 138
American Horse, 159
Antiquarian Bookstore, 164
Apache Books and Bedknobs, 138
Aquinas Bookstore, 151
Armchair Family Bookstore, 138
Art Mart, 149
Art of the Book, 141
Augustana College Bookstore, 55, 147
Baily School Supply, 146
Baker and Taylor, 81, 167
Baker's Bookstore, 156
Bartletts, 133
Fred N. Bay News Co., 138
Bear Pond, 83, 155, 156
Beechview News, 159
Beehive Specialty Foods, 166
Bellevue Book and Record Shop, 159
Bellevue Bookshop, 164
Best Buys, 148
Bethel Campus Store, 151
Birds and Bees, 138
Black Educational Center Bokstore, 138
Blocks Bookshop, 159
Blue Druid, 166
Bonneville News Co., 166
Book and Record Shop, 139
Book and Tea Shop, 134
Book Art, 158
Book Bazaar, 153
Book Cellar, The, 138
Book Cellar, The (Brattleboro), 156
Book Center, 162
Book City, 143
Book Craft, 166
Book Emporium, 152
Book Emporium (Champaign), 162
Book Exchange, 137
Book Exchange (Champaign),162
Book Exchange (La Cross), 148
Book Fair, 134
Book Gallery, The 141
Book Gallery (Sioux Falls), 147
Book Gallery, The (Manchester), 153
Book Haven, 138
Book Haven (Springfield), 152
Book House, The, 157
Book Mark, Inc., 160
Book Mart, 134
Book Mart (Buffalo), 158
Book Nook, 162
Book People, The, 134
Book Rack, The, 137
Book Sales Store, 158
Book Shack, 151

Book Vault, The, 139
Book and Yarn Barn, 155
Bookland, 141
Booklands, 28, 133
Books A-Go-Go, 118, 165
Books and Records, 144
Books International, 158
Books'n Tiques, 167
Books Primarily, 28, 133
Books Unlimited, 143
Bookseller, The, 142
Bookstore, 160
Bookstore, The, 163
Bookworld, 61, 151
Bookworm, The
Brathe's Bookstore, 149
Brian Thomas Books, 139
Broadway Bookstore, 148
Brown's Bookstore, 149
Browse House, 152
Bruggner's Town and Country, 151
Buckskin Press, The, 145
Buffalo Bulletin Bookstore, 146
SUNY-Buffalo Bookstore, 159
Buffalo Textbook Store, 158
Burlington News Agency, 155
By's Magazine Shop, 166
Cambridge Bookstore, 137
Campus Book Store, 164
Canyon Way Bookstore, 140
Card Shop, The, 162
Carr Stationery, 166
Carson Pirie Scott, 162
Cathedral Book Shop, 161
Central Book Exchange, 166
Chase's Cigar Store, 157
City Bookstore, 155
City News, 165
City News and Book, 164
City News and Book Co. (Lincoln), 164
Clark's Old Book Store, 141
Clearing House for Mind and Media, 53, 147
Climax Book Shop, 134
Cokesbury, 160, 163
College Store, 147
Columbus Wholesale Book Co., 161
Community News Stand, 151
Congress Book Shop, 154
Corl's, 136
Corner Bookstore, 155
Cottonwood Books, 166
Courtney's Books and Things, 147
Cove Bookstore, The, 154
Craig Office Supply, 140
Dakota News Agency, 55, 147
B. Dalton, 15, 55, 139, 141, 148
Deseret Bookstore, 119, 166
Dick's Book Exchange, 166
Distributor, The 62, 151
Drum C. Bookseller, 163
Dry Gulch Art Gallery, 52, 146
Duedall-Potts Stationary Store, 137
Eastern Book Company, 81, 154

Economy Book and Stationary, 157
Economy Bookstore, 91
Econ-o-read, 144
Elysian Fields, 164
Elysian Tree Metaphysical Store, 162
Epicurean Enterprises, 142
Epstein's, 109, 163
Erewhon, 36, 141
Everyday Bookshop, 156
Everyman's Booksote, 93, 158
Fairmount books, 157
Family Bookstore, 160
Feature Office Services, 148
Feminist Bookstore, The, 36
Follett's, University of Conn. Bookstore, 108, 152
Follett's U of I Book and Supply, 162
Freddy's Feed and Read, 143
Frost's book and Record, 166
Garden City News, 143
Garfield's 154
German Village, 161
Gill, J.K., 133, 139
Gimbel's, 160
Golden Mean bookstore, 132
Golden Tortoise, 136
Gonzaga University Bookstore, 142
Goodman's, 153
Good Book Stores, 161
John W. Graham Books, 36, 142
Grant Book and Stamp, 158
Grass Roots, 136
Great Books of the Western World, 139
Great Books of the Western World (Salt Lake City), 166
Green Dolphin, The, 139

Hallmark, 147
Hart-Albin Bookstore, 145
Hatch's Books, 145, 165
Haugen's, 143
Honig's Gift and Book Shop, 148
House of Crafts, 135
Hyatt's Bookstore, 132
Hyman's, 163
Id, The, 135
Inland Bookstore, 142
Interstate Periodical Distributors, 151
Iowa Book and Supply, 109, 163
Iowa, University of, Bookstore, 109, 163
Jay's Book Stall, 160
Johnson's Bookstore, 152—153
Jones' Bookshop, 81, 154
Journal, The, 153
Kauffman's, 101, 160
Kiva, The, 135
Kennebunkport Book, 154
Knudsen's Gift Shop, 155
Labor Book Center, 149
Lady Cybele's Cauldron, 149
Lamplighter, 163
Lange's Bookstore, 146
Larkin's Bookstore, 152

Lauriat's, 153
Libby's Bookstore, 158
Lion's Den, 161
Literary Lion, The, 135
Little Professor Book Center, 84, 93, 107, 156, 158, 161, 167
Logos Bookstore, 156
Logos Bookshop, 161
Logos Bookstore (Lincoln), 164
Long's, 161
Looking Glass Bookstore, 139
Main Street Bookstore, 159
Maine, University of, Portland, 155
Manchester Book Mart, 153
Manchester News Company, 153
Mandala, 156
Mart, The, 132
Mary's Books, 140
Mathew Benden & Co., 160
Mathews Bookstore, 164
McCarley's Books, 27, 132—133
McKay's Town/Campus Bookstore, 60, 148—149
Microcosm Bookstore, 149
Middle Earth Books, 26, 132
Miller and Paine, 165
Modern Age Bookstore, 152
Montana State University Bookstore, 37, 144
Montana, University of, Bookstore, 143
Moseley's, Inc., 61, 150
My Favorite Things, 162
National Book Mart, 160
Nebraska Bookstore, 165
Nebraska (University of, at Omaha) Bookstore, 164
Neimitz Book and Tobacco, 148
Nelson News, 164
Nelson's Books and Stationary, 150
News Bookstore, 148
North Idaho State College Bookstore, 142
North Node Bookstore, The, 155
Office Supply Co., The, 143
Onandaga News Agency, 157
Oregon State University Bookstore, 136
Oregon, University of, Bookstore, 29, 135
Our Place, 63, 152
Owl's Roost, 142
P.O. Newsstand, 144
Paperback Back Mart, 155
Paperback Booksmith, 153, 154
Paperback Exchange, 137
Paperback Exchange (Salt Lake City), 167
Paperbook Gallery, 161
Pastime Feminist Book Center, 142
Paul's, 150
Pauper's Bookstore, 53, 147
People's Bookstore, 159
Philips' Book and Office Supply, 144
Phoenix Books Ltd, 161

Pic-A-Book Store, 150
Pittsburgh (University of) Book Center, 160
Plainsmen Bookstore, 165

Pleiades, 137
Portland News Company, 155
Portland State University Bookstore, 140
Walt Powell Books, 140
Quality Bookstore, 166
R.S. Distributors, 167
Ralph's Books and Cards, 146
Randall's, 160
Reader's Den, 148
Read-Mor, 161
Readmore, 149
Reading Rack, 164
Rep Book Center, 140
Robeson's, 162
Rocky Mountain College Bookstore, 145
Sakti Book Shop, 150
Sax and Freyer, 144
Scott Kraus News Agency, 161
Shafer's Bookstore, 165
Sheridan College Bookstore, 145
Sheridan Stationery Co., 145
Shield's Book and Stationery, 141
Sign of Aquarius, 160
Sioux Falls College Bookstore, 55
F.W. Skelder, 160
Smith Family Bookstore, The, 135
Something Owl Bookstore, 140
Son of Koobdooga, 28, 136
Southern Oregon Book Co., 133
Spearfish Book, 146
Supply, The, 146
Swems, 28, 134
Syracuse Book Center, 91, 157
Syracuse University Bookstore, 92, 158
Tides, The, 167
Theosophical and Occult Books, 142
Tilden's, 156-157
Tony's Bookstore, 163
Trans Book Co., 27, 132
Two Worlds' Book Shoppe, 153
Ulbrich's, 93, 159
Unique Book Stall, 167
University Bookstore, 150
University Bookstore, The, 163
University Store (U. Vermont), 156
Used Bookstore, The, 108
Used Bookstore, The (Champaign), 162
Utah College Bookstore, 119-120, 166
Utah, University of, Bookstore, 119, 166
Varsity Book Exchange, 137
Varsity Book Exchange (Portland), 140
Vermont Bookshop, 156
Village Book Shop, 164
Vineyard, 161
Viterbo College Bookstore, 149
Volume 1, 140
Walden Books, 15, 16, 61, 136, 150, 152, 153, 159
Wall Drug, 54, 147
Wayne's Bookshop, 163
Weigelt Bros. Bookstore, 141
West Book Store, 165

Western Distributing Co., 160-161
Western Drug, 52, 146
Western Stationers, 147
Westerner, The, 146
Westside Books, 159
White Chapel Books, 144
Why Not R.E.A.D., 156
Willamette University Bookstore, 29, 137
Wilson's Pharmacy, 142-143
Wisconsin Independent News Department, 61, 151
Wisconsin, University of, LaCrosse, 59, 149
Woman's Place, 140
Worldwide, 162
Wyoming, University of, Bookstore, 118, 165
Youthtime Sword and Shield Bookstore, 159
Zion Bookstore, 120, 167
Zondervan Family Bookstore, 61, 151, 152

The American Dust Series

No. 1— **AMERICAN ODYSSEY** By Len Fulton with Ellen Ferber. A Bookselling Travelogue.

No. 2— **MOVING TO ANTARCTICA** A Women's Anthology edited by Margaret Kaminski.

No. 3— **CAPTIVE VOICES** An anthology of prose and poetry from Folsom Prison.

No. 4— **DARK OTHER ADAM DREAMING**, a novel by Len Fulton.

The American Dust Series is supported in part by a grant from the Literature Program of the National Endowment for the Arts.

Dustbooks

Small Press Information

INTERNATIONAL DIRECTORY OF LITTLE MAGAZINES AND SMALL PRESSES

DIRECTORY OF SMALL MAGAZINE/ PRESS EDITORS AND PUBLISHERS

SMALL PRESS RECORD OF BOOKS

   ONGOING *MONTHLY*

Write for complete list of titles.

Dustbooks

P.O. Box 1056,

Paradise, CA 95969

NOTES